Foundations of Modern Sociology Series

Alex Inkeles, *Editor*

The Sociology of Ideology, *Daniel Bell*
Science and Society, *Joseph Ben-David*
Deviance and Control, *Albert K. Cohen*
Modern Organizations, *Amitai Etzioni*
The Family, *William J. Goode*
Society and Population, *David M. Heer*
What Is Sociology? An Introduction to the Discipline and Profession, *Alex Inkeles*
Theory and Method in the Social Sciences, *Paul F. Lazarsfeld*
Person and Society: An Introduction to Social Psychology,
      Daniel J. Levinson and Alex Inkeles
The Sociology of Small Groups, *Theodore M. Mills*
Social Change, *Wilbert E. Moore*
The Sociology of Religion, *Thomas F. O'Dea*
Societies: Evolutionary and Comparative Perspectives, *Talcott Parsons*
The System of Modern Societies, *Talcott Parsons*
Community Social Structure, *Peter H. Rossi*
Changing Rural Societies, *Irwin T. Sanders*
The American School: A Sociological Analysis, *Patricia C. Sexton*
The Sociology of Economic Life, *Neil J. Smelser*
Social Stratification: The Forms and Functions of Inequality, *Melvin M. Tumin*

Foundations of Modern Sociology Series

the American school

A SOCIOLOGICAL ANALYSIS

Patricia Cayo Sexton, *New York University*

Prentice-Hall, Inc., *Englewood Cliffs, New Jersey*

In memory of Benjamin Cameron, Florence Winn, and Ethel Rogin; and in gratitude to my mother and my husband, Brendan, for encouragement and affection, to my colleagues Marvin Bressler, Erwin Smigel, Dan Dodson, and S. M. Miller for useful comments on the manuscript, and to Alex Inkeles for exceptionally kind, perceptive editorial guidance.

Prentice-Hall Foundations of Modern Sociology Series
Alex Inkeles, *Editor*

Current printing (last digit):
10 9 8 7 6 5 4

PRENTICE-HALL INTERNATIONAL, INC., London
PRENTICE-HALL OF AUSTRALIA, PTY., LTD., Sydney
PRENTICE-HALL OF CANADA, LTD., Toronto
PRENTICE-HALL OF INDIA PRIVATE LIMITED, New Delhi
PRENTICE-HALL OF JAPAN, INC., Tokyo

C

contents

v

schools: form and reformation

one

In preliterate society, life and learning were simple enough to be transmitted rather casually from one generation to the next. The complications of advancing civilization—development of the written and above all the printed word, the phenomenal growth of technical knowledge, industrialization, job specialization—required a special institution, the *school,* to teach the young what previous generations learned at home. It also required a place where children, no longer useful as farm hands, could be kept in custody while parents went to work. Creating this special institution often had the unfortunate side effect of separating education from life, learning from doing, and the school from society.

The school is not the only place where children learn. The media of learning have multiplied. While lively children are deposited in the school with "dead" knowledge for lengthening periods, the mass media and other knowledge creators and communicators have also appeared on the scene. *Education* and *the school* are now so identified, however, that the role of other media is overlooked. We need only reflect on the sources of our own learning and the forces shaping our personalities to recognize that we learn not only from teachers but from all our associations and experiences. Our knowledge and behavior derive not only from the school but from family, friends, religion, books, movies, television, and the social order. Even our language may come more from these sources than from the school. Learning goes on everywhere and at all times.

1

The contribution of schools to total learning is a matter of speculation rather than certain knowledge. With the competition of other media, we may learn little of significance in school. Nor is much known about interaction among the institutions that shape our lives—school, church, state, family, economy. Schools suffer perhaps more acutely from cultural lag than other institutions and often function more as an amputated than a healthy member of the social organism.

A vast topic itself, the school is set in an ever larger frame. Although most analysis has dealt with *microcosmic* aspects of the school, with classrooms, roles, and small units, in this book we will look at *macrocosmic* elements, at the larger, less explored, but more significant relationship of schools to society. In this relation, schools tend to be passive rather than active partners, guardians of tradition rather than initiators of change, dependent rather than independent variables. The school is a sub-system of the larger social system. Most of the processes and structures of the school which occupy the attention of researchers are simply mirrors reflecting, imperfectly, present or past images of the larger society. As delayed and touched-up versions of the original, they often conceal both the vices and the vitality of that real world.

On the other hand, schools have initiated some profound changes in the society. The sheer growth in size and power of educational institutions, particularly in higher education, has shaped the social structure. This growth, however, has been largely a product of demands in the *society* for more education, demands originating mainly with the disadvantaged in the population.

Usually the society directs the schools and decides, if it chooses, what they will do. When a society is shaken by new sources of social power, both inside and outside the nation, as the United States has been in the '60s, serious change can be expected in the schools, as in all social institutions.

Changing Contexts

The changing social context of the schools includes:

1. A world experiencing a triple revolution in scientific and military technology and in race relations. An era of American world dominance and growing commitment and competition. Increased influence of military and security agencies in national and international affairs, in educational institutions—especially institutions of higher learning—and in training people for military service. About half the adult males in the United States are or will be veterans of military training.

2. Rapid economic development, especially during wartime. From 1947 to 1963 median family income increased 50 percent in real dollars; by 1963, 93 percent of homes had TV, 62 percent of housing units were owner occupied, four in five households had telephones, about two out of three households had a car, far more than in the entire rest of the world. Increased leisure. Growing inequalities in the distribution of wealth despite improvement in absolute standards. Expansion of middle-class occupations and life-style. Growth in the public sector of the economy, and participation of new groups in the political system.

3. Growth in population, especially youth; nearly half the people who have ever lived in the United States were alive in the mid-1960's. Growth in the size of organizations and creation of an "organization society." Urbanization, population mobility, and new concern about "community."

4. Secularization of the society and increase in the social and social-action functions of religion. Amid changes, the continuing basic stability of the family.

2

While one in four marriages ends in divorce, the rate is not increasing. Declining function of the family as an agency for socializing the young. Changing role of women and greater participation in the life of the society; in 1940 about a third of women worked, in 1960 about 40 percent.

The strongest trend in the schools has been their growth in size and power. About one of three people is now part of the school system in one or another capacity. Teachers in public schools increased 50 percent during the decade ending in 1960. In that year they numbered 1,600,000, or more than three times the number of employees in the world's largest manufacturing corporation, General Motors. The teaching profession is expanding four times faster than the total population, and one out of five professionals is working for the public schools. Annual expenditure on the schools was about $23 billion in 1960, and over 50 percent of state and local payrolls go to the schools. In 1960, some three and a half million students attended college; by 1970 the figure will be over seven million. Masters degrees doubled from 1948 to 1962 and doctorates almost tripled.

Psyche and Social Order

Human and educational problems are illuminated more in examining the social order than in probing individual psyches, especially in times of rapid social change. Like the school, the psyche is shaped by the social system, so that stress in the former may often be traced to the latter.

The complexity of educational analysis lies in its relevance to all the social and behavioral sciences, covering topics from the individual psyche to the largest human organizations. The individual is, of course, a more manageable unit of study than a society. For this and other reasons, psychologists have dominated educational thought for several decades.[1] The psyche has been a primary concern of researchers, the immediate environment a secondary one, and the "social order" has been almost untouched.

The central figure of James Joyce's *Portrait of the Artist as a Young Man* identifies himself: "Stephen Dedalus, Class of Elements, Clongowes Wood College, Sallins, County Kildare, Ireland, Europe, the World, the Universe." The sociologist looks at the individual as the center of Dedalus' ever-widening circles of human society, stopping this side of the universe.

Sociology and Social Critics

The study of society came late to teacher training, and sociologists have, with important exceptions, generally neglected education. Sociology courses have abounded in schools of education but the influence of sociologists in teacher training has been far less than the influence of psychologists. In 1916 the first department of educational sociology was established at Columbia University, and by the end of the second World War there were 1,022 sociology courses listed in the catalogs of 162 teachers' colleges.[2]

Émile Durkheim, the great French sociologist, was concerned about the internal workings of the school, and its function in creating social equilibrium.

[1] In National Science Foundation listings of scientific and technical personnel, psychologists outnumber sociologists about six to one (16,800 to 2,700).

[2] Judson T. Landis, "The Sociological Curriculum and Teacher Training," *American Sociological Review* (1947) 12:113–116.

Like his American contemporaries, he wished to use the schools for social reform but, unlike them, he sought more *stability* rather than more *change*.[3] Concerned about *anomie* (normlessness) in modern society and the lack of concensus in urban life, he saw schools as a place where new primary relations and a new "community" could be formed to substitute for old rural norms. His more radical contemporaries, convinced that only a new social order could create a stable and equitable society, wanted the schools to create further social change. Then as now, opinions collided over *what* should be changed: individuals, institutions, or society.

Sociology was born of the modern ardor to improve society, wrote Albion Small in 1905.[4] Leftist and reformist politics dominated German sociological interest in the schools after World War I, and many eminent American social observers were of this tradition. Lester Ward, early American sociologist, once wrote ". . . education is the mainspring of all progress; it is the piston of Civilization." Ward proposed numerous school reforms including rejection of IQ tests and all constricting notions about innate intelligence.[5] Horace Mann believed that "It may be safely affirmed that the common school, improved and energized as it can easily be, may become the most effective and benignant of all the forces of civilization." [6]

Philosopher John Dewey in 1897 wrote, "I believe that education is the fundamental method of social progress and reform." [7] The American progressive education movement, derived from his teaching, was politically "liberal," though less radical than groups that wished the schools to create a "new social order." [8] Debates of the period took place in a context of rising political movements and socialist dissent; they influenced not the schools but some articulate educators, social critics, and their later disciples.[9]

Dewey wanted the school to change, to move closer to the learner's life experience, and away from accepted dogma and obsolete knowledge:

> I assume that amid all uncertainties there is one permanent frame of reference: namely, the organic connection between education and personal experience; or, that the new philosophy of education is committed to some kind of empirical and experimental philosophy.[10]

The school should "grow gradually out of the home life; it should take up and continue the activities with which the child is already familiar in the home." [11]

Among the distortions attributable to some of Dewey's followers was their substitution of "permissive" for "progressive," their inclination to enshrine the often whimsical "authority" of the child, and their tendency to overemphasize social relations as against learning and inquiry, based perhaps on Dewey's early

[3] Émile Durkheim, *Education and Sociology* (New York: The Free Press of Glencoe, 1956).

[4] Albion Small, *General Sociology* (Chicago: University of Chicago Press, 1905).

[5] Lester Ward, unpublished manuscript, p. 311, reported by Elsa P. Kimball, *Society and Education* (New York: Columbia University Press, 1932), p. 216.

[6] Horace Mann, "Physical, Moral and Religious Education," Twelfth Annual Report, reprinted in Bernard Johnson (ed.), *Issues in Education, An Anthology of Controversy* (Boston: Houghton Mifflin, 1964), p. 377.

[7] John Dewey, "My Pedogogic Creed," in *Issues in Education, op cit.*, p. 220.

[8] Lawrence Cremin, *The Transformation of the School, Progressivism in American Education, 1786–1957* (New York: Knopf, 1961).

[9] John Dewey was identified with the democratic socialist movement while others of his day were closer to other political and radical groups.

[10] John Dewey, "Traditional vs. Progressive Education," in *Issues in Education, op. cit.*, p. 225.

[11] Dewey, "My Pedagogic Creed," in *Issues in Education, op. cit.*, p. 216.

4

view that the true center of learning was not traditional subjects "but the child's own social activities." [12]

Obsolescence

A central theme in the history of educational criticism is the isolation of schools from society and the consequent obsolescence of both method and substance of instruction.

Late in the nineteenth century, the English philosopher and sociologist Herbert Spencer insisted that instruction should deal with the scientific and useful, rather than with the aesthetic, the traditions of scholasticism, or the experience and needs of the child—as followers of Rousseau and Comenius were suggesting then and Dewey later. "Throughout his after-career a boy, in nine cases out of ten, applies his Latin and Greek to no practical purpose," Spencer wrote.

> If we inquire what is the real motive for giving boys a classical education, we find it to be simply conformity to public opinion. . . . The births, deaths, and marriages of kings, and other like historic trivialities, are committed to memory, not because any direct benefits can possibly result from knowing them, but because society considers them parts of a good education. . . .[13]

In this view conspicuous consumption—intellectual rather than material—was the motive for traditional education.

> By the accumulation of wealth, by style of living, by beauty of dress, by display of knowledge or intellect, each tries to subjugate others, and so aids in weaving that ramified network of restraints by which society is kept in order. It is not the savage chief only who, in formidable warpaint with scalps at his belt, aims to strike awe into his inferiors; it is not only the belle who, by elaborate toilet, polished manners, and numerous accomplishments, strives to 'make conquests,' but the scholar, the historian, the philosopher, use their acquirements to the same end.[14]

Direct utility of knowledge is scarcely more regarded by schools "than by the barbarian when filing his teeth and straining his nails." [15]

> We yield to none, in the value we attach to aesthetic culture and its pleasures. . . . So far from thinking that the training and gratification of the tastes are unimportant, we believe that the time will come when they will occupy a much larger share of human life than now. . . . However important it may be, it must yield precedence to those kinds of culture which bear more directly upon the duties of life.[16]

While this which we call civilization could never have arisen had it not been for science, science forms scarcely an appreciable element in what men consider civilized training.[17]

Obsolescence is also a product of ambiguity about educational goals. When goals are unclear, educators are uncertain about what to teach, researchers about what to measure, and all cling safely to tradition. In general, educators have clashed over the emphasis to be placed on the needs of society as contrasted

[12] Dewey, "My Pedagogic Creed," in *Issues in Education, op. cit.,* p. 217.
[13] Herbert Spencer, "What Knowledge Is of Most Worth?" reprinted in *Issues in Education, op. cit.,* p. 307.
[14] *Ibid.,* p. 308. [15] *Ibid.,* p. 308.
[16] *Ibid.,* p. 314. [17] *Ibid.,* p. 316.

5

with the needs of the child—the need for economic and technical versus social and aesthetic development—the importance of subject matter and intellectual training as contrasted with moral, social, physical, and personality development.

Ideology and Reform

All societies use the schools for ideological instruction, to transmit core values to the young and to teach order and loyalty to the society. In this, societies seem to be arranged along a continuum of ideologic pedagogy. Those with little national consensus, elaborate and rigid ideological dogma, and a concentrated power structure are usually found at one end of the continuum. Our schools would undoubtedly fall at the other end. The American value system is, except in crisis, a *relatively* open one, pragmatic, flexible, and uncodified into dogmas or documents guiding thought and behavior. Such pragmatism gives the society its remarkable capacity for adaptation and development, but it is dysfunctional when it fails to integrate the society and when it encourages excessive ambiguity about goals and norms, especially in the young.

Schools in the United States, as in other Judeo-Christian societies, were founded by religious groups for the purpose of religious instruction. The Massachusetts Act of 1647, making public education compulsory for the first time, was in fact written by church officials to provide vocational training and to help "delude Satan." In some countries religious groups still dominate public education. In Spain, Protestants have been forbidden by law to establish schools, and in much of Latin America, church schools are supported by public funds. In Africa and other developing areas, schools are still largely run by religious orders.

Latin and the classical tradition dominated the secondary school curriculum during the colonial period in America, and science and technology were introduced only over the opposition of both religious and pedagogical groups. The early colleges were theological centers. The influence of scholastic theology at Harvard is revealed in this thesis topic: "When Balaam's Ass Spoke, Was There Any Change in Its Organs?" (1731), or "When the Shadow Went Back on the Sun-Dial of Hezekiah, Did the Shadows Go Back on All Sun-Dials?"

Because of ideological ambiguities in both school and society, philosophers have played a leading part in educational discussions, particularly in debates over issues such as "totalitarian" versus "democratic" education. In institutions where goals are clear, as profits are for businesses, philosophy has no role.

Social reformers have generally failed to influence school practices. Dewey's experimental method was, for example, enthusiastically greeted by many teachers who did not know how to use it and who reverted to the easy tradition of textbook memorization. Yet desire for reform seems as endemic to behavioral science as to the American temperament. Psychologists explore learning and behavior with a view to improving human performance; similarly, many sociologists study society with a view to improving its performance.

The macrocosmic view of education is often associated with advocacy of radical social change. "If you study social organizations in detail," said Raymond Aron, French sociologist: "you will find something to improve everywhere. In order to seek a revolution—that is, a total upheaval—you must assume an overall viewpoint, take up a synthetic model, define the essence of a given society, and reject that essence.[18]

[18] Raymond Aron, *Main Currents in Sociological Thought*, trans. Richard Howard and Helen Weaver (New York: Basic Books, 1965), pp. 5–6.

schools: form and reformation

Educational reform has been diverted by the microscopic perspective of those engaged in educational research and development and by their myopic focus on classroom processes. A macrocosmic view and the location of pressure points in the *social system* and the *school system* may produce the change (and the funds and attention) that are needed to improve classroom performance.

The social scientist legitimately derives the given values of a society—such as freedom and democracy, equality, material progress—and notes the extent to which they are observed in its institutions. In the process, conclusions may be drawn and hypotheses developed which may aid social policy decisions and guide efforts to realize these values in the operation of social institutions.

Crisis and Conflict

American schools, once the most placid of institutions, have been torn by internal strife and subjected to continuing attack. Civil rights struggles and rising expectations have directed the hostility of large minorities against the schools. It is charged that the schools fail to reach the "disadvantaged," to make them even functionally literate. The old system of local control and local financing is dissolving as the society becomes more national and more urban. Spreading affluence, automobile ownership among the young, the pervasiveness of TV, and other distractions crowd out school as a focus of teen-age interest.

New technology and computerization create all but insuperable tasks of maintaining a modern curriculum, at the same time that they simplify other tasks. They make it more difficult for schools to teach relevant job skills, and they force large employers to assume more responsibility for training workers, especially the highly skilled. For the first time (in the Job Corps) the instruction of the young was turned over by government to private enterprise, and the United States Office of Education has granted funds to private groups for research and development.

Schools have been shaken by teacher demands for union recognition in the major cities of the nation. Before the end of the 1960's probably a majority of teachers will be represented in collective bargaining either by the American Federation of Teachers, or the increasingly militant affiliates of the National Education Association. Under external and internal assault, the authority of traditional school leadership has been undermined. The principle of federal aid having been established, federal intervention inevitably will follow, as it has in civil rights enforcement and in setting rules for new federal programs.

Burgeoning college populations limit the state university's ability to offer opportunity to low-income students. Increasing demand also contributes to the phenomenal growth of community and junior colleges, which inevitably will alter the course of education in coming decades.

Colleges of education have been forced to give ground to liberal arts faculties, and to modify their teacher training curriculum. Definitions of the "profession of teaching" have been redrawn, new avenues of professionalism established, and new school "aide" occupations created.

Students and youth have become articulate and organized critics of education, and new groups are becoming "participants" in the education process.

Social scientists studying the American education system operate against a tapestry of chaos and dissolution woven of these obtrusive facts. A commentary on the sociology of education, then, becomes a critique; but only in the light of understanding education's agonizing difficulties is it possible to look at and evaluate the school as a social institution.

7

Order and Priority

During periods of rapid social change, texts in the sociology of education quickly become obsolete. During most periods, however, the subject of social and racial *stratification* has been central to the study of schools in society. The school stratifies the population into "quality" layers and selects the society's elite as well as its rejects. Because of this social sorting, the issue of mass versus elite education has become a pivotal one in the American school, as has the school's role in promoting mass mobility.

Sociologists have stressed stratification in the schools more than other subjects. A group of 168 instructors of educational sociology courses indicated these subjects as most appropriate to their courses: "social status" (85 percent of respondents); "social mobility" (85 percent); "social change" and "social conflict" (84 percent); "social class structure" (84 percent)—all of which are part of the study of social stratification. No similar stress was given to "power" and, in fact, only 40 percent said that "politics" should be a subject of concern. Only 54 percent felt that "economics" was relevant; 55 percent felt that "international social problems" should be included; and 51 percent voted for consideration of "urban and rural society." [19]

Since the school stands, like St. Peter, at the gateway to upper levels of a stratified society, it is a temptation to give this issue top priority. Yet during the present era, two other elements of the social system seem to take priority over stratification. These are *power* and *economics,* or the political and economic systems which together greatly influence the production and distribution of wealth and status in school and society.

The strongest threads contained in this volume are:

1. The central role of power in school and society, and the controls exercised within the educational system by higher education and by administrators, bureaucracies, and traditional business values.

2. The role of the school in equalizing educational opportunity and the gross inequities existing in both school and society.

3. The determining effect on all social institutions, including the schools, of the economic system and material production.

4. The role of values and ideology in shaping social and educational goals, and in making both more vital and efficient.

5. The inefficiency of the schools as large-scale organizations and the lessons to be learned from more successful organizations.

6. The city as the explosive locale of the contemporary American school.

7. The obsolescence of schools, their essential isolation from society and all its sub-systems, and the central need to promote all varieties of interaction between school and society.

8. The promise of research and development and of scientific social research for the future of the American school.

This book is not a dictionary of concepts. Rather, it is an effort to analyze some of the significant characteristics and problems in the schools using whatever sociological concepts and tools are relevant to the task. Many rather common concepts do not seem very useful and will, therefore, be omitted; unfortunately, other concepts are needed that are not yet clearly defined.

[19] Richard Gjermund Hoyme, *Educational Sociology,* a dissertation presented to the faculty of the School of Education, the University of California, January, 1961.

schools: form and reformation

power, I:
society
and
higher education
two

The expansion of schools in size and strategic roles has greatly increased their power in society. At the same time, the monopoly of public schools over education is being threatened. Business, labor, religious, and citizen groups, as well as other public agencies, have entered the field and set up programs in job training, education, research and development, and community education.

Graduate schools stand at the apex of the school power pyramid, being at once the loftiest and fastest-growing. They have absorbed much of the power of undergraduate schools which, in turn, had absorbed much of the secondary school's influence. "Over any considerable period of time, the men who teach in America's leading graduate schools," says Christopher Jencks, "determine for the rest of us not only what is true and what is false but, in large measure, what is 'done' and 'not done.' " [1] Higher education is a brain center of technological and scientific development. Not only does it train the professionals employed in other institutions which conduct research and development, but also increasingly initiates innovation through its own research and development operations.

[1] Chrisopher Jencks, "Who Should Control Education?" *Dissent* (March–April, 1966), 150.

9

Power of Schools

Since it helps select society's elites, higher education also dominates the society's stratification system. Not long ago in the American past, the illiterate self-made man was not uncommon. Now the ambitious face a long series of educational hurdles, the highest of which are set by graduate schools. Educational requirements for almost all jobs, justifiably or not, have been raised, and even business elites, formerly composed of the self-made and self-educated, are now being recruited from graduate schools. The power of the diploma varies, however, with the supply of skilled manpower. During the great depression, when demand was low and supply high, college degrees were required of dime-store clerks.

Higher education has always influenced the public schools. With its phenomenal expansion in the first half of the twentieth century, the secondary school sometimes tried to assert its independence of the academic requirements and historic dominance of higher education, but the subsequent rapid growth of colleges more than balanced the scale again.

The secondary school has usually stood mid-way between the *child*-centered elementary school and the *subject*-centered university, leaning first one way and then another. It has tended to balance the elementary school's "child centered" curriculum by emphasizing subject matter and content, and the needs of professionals as distinct from the needs of children. Partly because of its larger male faculty and older student body, relations between staff and students have been less "nurturant" and more "professional" than in lower schools. On the other hand, it has been more maternal and protective than higher educational institutions and more interested in students and less in scholarship than the colleges.

As higher education extends its size and power, its control over the curriculum of secondary and elementary schools increases, and its standards are passed down even to early primary grades. Colleges also influence lower schools through training of administrators, teachers, researchers, and other school professionals.[2]

The collective influence of higher education is exercised through organizations such as the American Council on Education, dominated by large public and private prestige institutions and operating to influence private foundation and federal policy. Other organizations of varying influence are the Association of Land Grant Colleges and Universities, the American Association of University Professors, the Association of American Colleges, the Association for Higher Education, the American Association of Junior Colleges, and the regional accrediting associations.

Among the most powerful organizations in higher education are those that set standards, groups such as the Educational Testing Service which controls the College Board and other exams, the accrediting associations that grant college accreditation, and the state and private bodies that control professional training and certification.

---

[2] Campbell and Bunnell, in interviews with administrators and teachers, found that the four national organizations most influential with secondary schools were all concerned with college entry: National Science Foundation, National Merit Scholarship Program, the National Defense Education Act, the College Entrance Examination Board. See Ronald F. Campbell and Robert A. Bunnell, *Nationalizing Influences on Secondary Education* (Chicago: University of Chicago, Midwest Administration Center, 1963).

10

Power of Knowledge

Power is obtained through access to significant information. In this sense knowledge *is* power. Those who are power*less* invariably lack strategic information and those who are power*ful* attain and retain their power only insofar as such information is available to them. Computerization and easy retrieval of information are likely to alter the power structure of society, giving those with access to these sources additional increments of power. Higher education, the producer and distributor of much advanced and strategic information, is a guardian of the computerized future.

Education and information give power to the powerless. In the mid-nineteenth century, Horace Mann wrote, "Surely nothing but universal education can counterwork this tendency to the domination of capital and the servility of labor. . . . If education be equally diffused, it will draw property after it, for such a thing cannot happen that, an intelligent and practical body of men should be permanently poor. . . . Education, then, beyond all other devices of human origin, is the greater equalizer of the conditions of men—the balance-wheel of the social machinery." [3]

The wider distribution of knowledge which men can use to control their environment is essential to the democratization of social power. Although educational institutions stratify and create elites, they also democratize by offering information and opportunity to the less powerful, and by introducing new people and ideas into the traditional elite.

Although educational institutions and the knowledge they develop and disseminate are becoming more strategic in the society, they face a formidable competitor for public funds in the military-industrial complex. Compared to the priority given defense expenditures, especially during war, the priority of schools and social services is low. The future of the schools depends, then, upon the relaxation of international tensions, the assignment of high priority and massive expenditures to education, and the ability of the American economy to stabilize at high growth rates during peacetime in order to generate funds for schools.

Society

"Power," said Robert MacIver, "is the agent, indeed the very being, of all that happens on earth and over the whole universe." [4] However pantheistic the nature of power, it is the essence of the social order in school and society. Those who have the power to make important decisions usually do not advertise it, for fear that it will be taken away or that others will try to influence those decisions. Because of its essentially concealed and sensitive nature, conspiratorial fantasies about monolithic "power structures" are woven, as well as opposite fantasies about the total dispersal of power.

Power is as central in the social and educational systems as it is, in a physical form, in the industrial system. The most dramatic changes in each system derive from new sources of power. Mechanical power, generated by new sources of energy, created modern industry. It also changed the structure of society by moving people from the land to the industrial cities where the new

[3] Horace Mann, "Physical, Intellectual, Moral and Religious Education," *Issues in Education, op. cit.,* p. 380.

[4] Robert M. MacIver, *Power Transformed* (New York: Macmillan, 1964), p. 75.

"power structure" consisted of owners and managers rather than landlords. The advance of urban industrial democracy, however, tended to diffuse somewhat the power once held by small elites, a diffusion that has profoundly affected the schools.

Power, according to Robert Bierstedt, depends on the social organization, resources, and numbers of people.[5] That is, a large group, with strong and effective organization and abundant resources, will command more power than other groups. Those who have held dominant power in the schools have attained their positions through membership in influential organizations, through personal wealth and status, and through knowledge about people and affairs of both community and school. The power of *insurgent* groups seems to lie in their numbers, discontent, ideological energy, and, eventually, their capacity to organize. Usually they are deficient in resources and established social organization.

"Integration" and "coercion" theories of social power are counterposed by Ralf Dahrendorf.[6] The first sees society as an integrated system held in equilibrium by certain recurrent processes; the second regards society as a system held together by compulsion, and producing continuous change and conflict. Such views shift with the times. During periods of rapid social change, when new power groups are rising, it is natural to see conflict rather than equilibrium as basic to the social structure. Conflict is also more pervasive in the developing than in the advanced societies where prosperity and the coercive power of the state tend to temper rebellion. The decades of the '50's and '60's in American education were characterized by change, conflict, and compulsion, generated by the discontent of the disadvantaged, rather than by equilibrium.

The study of power, says Richard Schermerhorn, reverses the emphasis of the equilibrium theory "by assuming that change is the starting point and that order or equilibrium is a by-product of the ceaseless quest for power by individuals, groups, institutions, and nations." [7] We lean to the coercion theory of power, where relevant. Conflict and change, within some limits, will be seen as healthy rather than impaired functions of the social organism. When schools have changed they have done so because citizens have sought power and status through their services. Because of their essential isolation from power struggles in the society, schools have until recent times changed very little; more accurately, in fact, they have *grown* rather than *changed*. As traditional institutions, they have been proud of their "stability." Clearly the extraordinary "equilibrium" of educational institutions, in a rapidly changing society, has been a symptom of sickness, not of health.

Capitalism and Corporate Power

Rise of Corporate Power

Disproportionate power is, or can be, wielded in school and society by wealth-holding groups. Capitalism and corporate power, which have been virtually synonymous with the American economic system, have tended to dominate most of the society's institutions—directly, through intermediaries, or through general extension of the business ethic.

[5] Robert Bierstedt, "An Analysis of Social Power," *American Sociological Review* (December, 1950), 15:730–738.
[6] Ralf Dahrendorf, *Class and Class Conflict in Industrial Society* (Stanford: Stanford University Press, 1959).
[7] Richard A. Schermerhorn, *Society and Power* (New York: Random House, 1961), p. 14.

The early years of capitalism, before it settled into corporate bureaucracy, were characterized by upheaval and a rapacity of acquisition that set violent counter forces in motion. Industrialization shook up the old rural way of life, created dreary urban slums, and imposed a harsh existence on workingmen. R. H. Tawney, the eminent British economic historian, said of its morality and public spirit: "Modern capitalism is absolutely irreligious, without internal union, without much public spirit, often, though not always, a mere congeries of possessors and pursuers." [8] Protestantism, according to Tawney, provided the ethical and religious foundation on which capitalism was built. Tawney and others believed that the articulation of the so-called Protestant ethic was a response to the need for a moral rationalization of capitalist virtues such as hard work, individual responsibility, usury, thrift, and acquisitiveness.

Socialism, as a response to the liabilities of rising capitalism, has been in the wind for several centuries. Early spokesmen for a system that emphasized a public ethic and public controls included sociologists Auguste Comte, Claude Saint-Simon, and others. Many of their ideas have become a part of the American heritage, embodied in such documents as the Declaration of Independence, and have stimulated native American radicalism.

Like the doctrines of capitalism and democratic socialism, Marxism is relevant to modern schools and society for many reasons, including the probability that a majority of teachers in the world regard themselves as Marxists, while millions of school children religiously read *The Communist Manifesto*, which asserts that capitalism substituted for former rule by feudal lords, "naked, shameless, direct, brutal exploitation . . . veiled by religious and political illusions." The last plank of its platform calls for free universal education, an idea borrowed from the Western democracies—one in which the U.S.S.R. invests at a higher rate than the United States.[9]

Early capitalism seems only vaguely to resemble the new corporate power, significant parts of which have accommodated to liberal pressure and developed a sense of responsibility to the whole society. "The economic and technological triumphs of the past few years," said Henry Ford, II, one corporate spokesman, "have not solved as many problems as we thought they would. What really counts, when we measure social progress is not the ingenuity of technology or the growth of national product, but the quality of our society and our individual lives. . . . Those who are more fortunate, including the leaders of the business world, have a duty to their country and themselves to join the war on poverty, on discrimination, on ignorance, on unemployment." [10]

Industrialization, carried on in the United States by the "capitalist class," caused much human and social wreckage but it also spurred economic development and made political democracy, prosperity, and modern society possible. More important, industrialization stimulated the organization of workers which, in turn, gave them new social power, the ability to divert some of the resources of the society to human needs, and the means with which to buy and demand education for their children. The economic and political power of these insurgent groups tempered the early Protestant ethic and was instrumental in directing some elements of the corporate world toward a more social ethic.

[8] R. H. Tawney, *Religion and the Rise of Capitalism* (New York: Harcourt, Brace, 1926).

[9] Other planks call for abolition of private land-holdings and rights of inheritance; nationalization of banks and credit, communication and transportation; extension of state factories; heavy graduated income tax; "equal liability of all to labor"; gradual abolition of the distinction between town and country by redistribution of population; abolition of child labor and "combination of education with industrial production."

[10] Henry Ford, II, *New York Times* (May 4, 1966), p. 1.

13

"Devil" and "diffusion" views of power are at opposite ends of a continuum. At one end, power in the United States is seen as highly concentrated and at the other as fully diffused. "As things are today," writes David Riesman, "most observers seem unwilling to take a straight look at the amorphous distribution of power in America." [11] On the other side, C. Wright Mills saw a highly concentrated "power elite." [12] In the 'fifties, he wrote that in the United States "major national power now resides in the economic, the political, and the military domains." Other institutions are, "off to the side in modern history," he asserted. "Families and churches and schools adapt to modern life; governments and armies and corporations shape it. . . ." [13] Whether or not they make such decisions, he said, "is less important than the fact that they do occupy such pivotal positions: their failure to act . . . is itself an act that is often of greater consequence than the decisions they make." [14] Although Mills' view seems extreme, economic power does appear to be highly concentrated. "The idea of a really wide distribution of economic ownership," he contended, "is a cultivated illusion; at the very most 0.2 or 0.3 percent of the adult population own the bulk, the pay-off shares, of the corporate world." [15]

Bernard Nossiter claims that "for all the nation's much vaunted richness and diversity, it appears that a comparative handful, the managers and boards of a hundred or so corporations, are in control. . . . But most of them resist with all of their considerable strength any sharing of their power, even with the friendliest of governments." [16]

The managers, those who possess power without property, have come into command positions in the corporation, as they have in the schools and other

[11] David Riesman, *The Lonely Crowd* (New Haven: Yale University Press, 1951), p. 253.

[12] C. Wright Mills, *The Power Elite* (New York: Oxford University Press, 1957). Floyd Hunter found that: "Membership in the top brackets of one of the stable economic bureaucracies is the surest road to power"; in one Southern city he found fear of change in the top power group, refusal to share responsibility even though the small elite could not handle all the work, and a low level of civic interest. Floyd Hunter, *Community Power Structure* (Chapel Hill, N.C.: University of North Carolina). Vidich and Bensman report that in a small town in New York final public decisions were made by one business man and public spending was minimal, roads and schools being the main public expenses. The town received from the state about twenty times more than it paid in taxes. The political influence and values of such small towns have shaped much of American life and schools. As political power passes from these towns to the metropolitan areas, profound changes in national culture will occur. Arthur J. Vidich and Joseph Bensman, *Small Town in Mass Society* (Princeton, N.J.: Princeton University Press, 1958). In a small midwestern town, Joseph Lyford found that rural people were becoming less insular and more convinced that public initiatives are needed to solve the problems of the farmer and the small town. Joseph P. Lyford, *The Talk in Vandalia: The Life of an American Town* (New York: Harper Colophon Books, 1962), p. 10.

[13] *Ibid.*, p. 6.

[14] *Ibid.*, p. 4.

[15] Seligman reports that only 6 percent of corporations in 1959 had assets worth over a million dollars, yet they accounted for 70 percent of corporate receipts and 55 percent of national income. "All the small corporations and individual proprietorships and partnerships together do not have the impact on our economic well-being that a relatively few large corporations have." Ben B. Seligman, "The American Corporation: Ideology and Reality," *Dissent* (Summer 1964), II:316–327. In 1953, according to Lampman, 1.6 percent of the nation's adult population owned 82.4 percent of publicly held stock shares. Robert J. Lampman, *Share of Top Wealth Holders in National Wealth*, National Bureau of Economic Research (Princeton, N.J., 1962).

[16] Bernard Nossiter, "New Folklore of Capitalism," *Progressive* (September, 1962), 14.

institutions. Corporate power also tends to dominate, though not monopolize, the mass media—including radio, television, and the newspaper, magazine, and book-publishing industries.

Political Power

Economic and political power elites have, to a considerable extent, interlocked. "Civil government," wrote Adam Smith, "so far as it is instituted for the security of property, is in reality instituted for the defense of the rich against the poor. . . ." [17] In democracies, however, government serves many masters. Usually it is an intermediary between conflicting groups. Economic power is highly concentrated in the United States and the impact of that power is felt in the political system where money and influence are used to affect the decisions of politicians and voters. The possessors of economic power are not always effective. Certainly, many reforms have been made over their opposition. In fact, the basic nature of the system has radically altered, though the economically powerful would have had it otherwise.

Coalitions

Power is manifest in coalitions formed in response to specific needs or general interests. American medicine successfully organized in behalf of the economic interests of private physicians through a coalition with drug companies and others who sought support from doctors. That coalition was weakened by middle-class objections to the rising costs of medicine and the prospect to drug companies of expanded sales through public support of medicine. The coalition having been weakened, it became vulnerable to another, composed largely of organized labor, the older population, and others who could not afford medical care.

Power coalitions continually form and fall apart. In a society where economic and social expectations are relatively high and social arrangements infinitely complex, the immediate goals of many groups often run counter to their long-range ideological perspectives. Thus also with the schools. Large corporate and industrial enterprise, which has traditionally opposed, or been indifferent to many forms of school aid, is, based on its own needs, a potential supporter of an expanding educational system. Operating nationally, it is driven to greater concern with the stability of the whole society, and does not want it torn apart by strife. Since its wealth and power are great, it sometimes can take the long view and make concessions to disaffected groups without feeling its own position threatened. It may, therefore, support the schools out of a desire to hold the society together, as well as an interest in educating citizens.

Smaller businessmen can less afford the larger view. Increases in property and income taxes often threaten their status and standard of living. Psychologically, they are more threatened by the upward thrust of previously submerged groups. Inner contradictions in the coalition of business forces that for generations dominated the "locally controlled" American school system have created great fissures in recent times, as some of the more powerful business interests gradually withdrew opposition to federally aided education and other programs. The alliance between this group and smaller businessmen who have traditionally controlled the local, and therefore highly restrictive, school system has been weakened and made vulnerable to the coalition of civil rights groups, labor organizations, academics, aspiring lower-middle and working-class elements who have sought to force the schools to become more responsive to

[17] Adam Smith, *The Wealth of Nations* (New York: Modern Library, 1937).

their needs.[18] In addition, some powerful industries, such as publishing and construction, have had a direct economic stake in school expansion and have favored public assistance to this end.

In general, corporate power has, in the past, been as indifferent to problems of the nation's schools as it has to other social problems. It has opposed or neglected community planning and spending which might meet human needs and provide such simple amenities as clean air and water. It has assumed that school authority was safely deposited with allies on local school boards and among school administrators.

Early capitalism wanted only that the schools produce an adequately trained, hard working, and tractable work force—without frills. It wanted low school taxes and a structure which would place a minimal tax load on industry. It wanted a "power structure" and system of controls in the schools that was safe, traditional, and stable. That position, however, has been considerably altered. The "business community" has become less monolithic and more concerned about a national society, and its early Protestant ethic has been mellowed to some extent by a later social one. Having abandoned its coalition with local and states' rights groups on some issues, it has been more prepared to play a role in improving the American school and creating a national society.

The United States has generally been strong in the private economic sector and relatively weak in the public sector, where complex problems have often been left exclusively to voluntary associations and private initiative. Consequently, in the areas of greatest strain—the schools and cities—there has been a scarcity of either public or private initiative.

Higher Education

External Control

Top decision-makers in colleges and universities are the governing boards. These generally appointed boards are, even in public institutions, composed largely of business and professional people. Important alumni contributors and policy-influencers usually have similar origins. Though some faculties and administrators are relatively independent, all are finally responsible to governing boards. In some institutions faculty cannot attend board meetings, and few faculty members or students have ever served on governing boards. This concentration of authority has been a growing source of conflict.

"Since all legal authority rests in the board," writes Howard Mumford Jones, "its members may abolish or alter parts of a university or invent new ones with or without the consent of the faculty, and may also promulgate rules governing the lives of students and of faculty members that may or may not be consonant with the real purpose of the institutions." [19] "Whatever the society wants," said Robert Maynard Hutchins, "the university will do, provided

[18] Larger business interests lost to smaller ones at the Republican National Convention in 1964, and in the national elections that year they were either neutralized or joined a coalition that favored expanded education. The defeat of the Republican candidate, who embodied smaller business political goals, opened the doors to federal intervention in schools and society. The interests of power groups and coalitions may be seen in Congressional voting records where the most significant decisions on national issues are made. The voting record in the Senate of the 89th Congress, for example, on the Elementary and Secondary School Act, the first major piece of federal school legislation was: Democrats, 55 votes for, and 4 against the Act; Republicans, 18 for and 14 against.

[19] Howard Mumford Jones, "The Meaning of a University," *The Atlantic* (November, 1965), 158.

16

it gets the money to pay for it. And it is not even what the society wants. It is what the most vocal and well-heeled pressure groups demand." [20]

Internal Control

Most university faculties have greater decision-making power in their institutions than public school teachers, though the influence of both groups is growing. The rapid growth of educational institutions, teacher shortages, and the organization of teachers have added to the power of professionals.

The "power establishment" in higher learning, as in public education, has been challenged to some extent by both faculty and students. Professors, especially in community colleges and public universities, have joined the American Federation of Teachers, a trade union, to engage in collective bargaining and strike action. Their professional organization, the American Association of University Professors, has become more active, and both faculty and students have organized around economic (salary, tuition), academic (free speech), power (control in the institution), and political (peace, civil rights) issues.

In other countries, faculty and student activity is commonplace. As early as the thirteenth century, in Italy, students formed guilds for protection against merchants who sold them goods, and then against their professors. They demanded that the professors, whom they selected and paid themselves, begin and end lectures on time, stick to the subject, and eliminate excess verbiage. Later, the merger of student and professor guilds founded the University of Bologna.

Except for the token authority of most student councils, students in the United States have been outside the university power structure, even though they are the paying consumers of education. This powerlessness has limited the feedback from students about the quality of their education, as well as the experience of students in democratic processes. It has been functional to institutions to the degree that they have operated without breakdown and in conformity with established rules and standards. Greater options are permitted college students in selection of institutions and courses than students in lower schools, but choices are still essentially restrictive.

Youth—idealistic, restless, often confused, and lacking family responsibilities—is a prime source of resistance and rebellion. In many places, youth has ignited social action movements. Most of these movements perish as their youthful leaders mature and conditions change, but when permanent organizations are built, such as in trade unions or in revolutions that come to power, the effect has been more profound.[21] In the United States conflict over civil rights and peace moved many students out of the "silent generation" into campus action during the mid-sixties. Student action often opposed "bureaucracy," irrelevant studies, and favored popular "participation." Often such activities were more an assertion of nonconformist style than ideology or serious political understanding.

American youth became an object of special concern during the 'sixties when their numbers were proportionately larger than ever before. That this swollen youth population produced so little strain in the society can perhaps

[20] Robert Maynard Hutchins, "Fund for the Republic," *Center Diary*: 14 (September–October, 1966).

[21] The age of joining revolutionary parties of 163 communist leaders hit a steep peak at 17 and 18 years, and the age of first revolutionary activity hit a peak a little later. J. Davis, "A Study of One Hundred and Sixty-Three Outstanding Communist Leaders," *American Sociological Review, Papers and Proceedings* (1929), 42–53.

17

be attributed to the scarcity of causes for discontent. Generally, youth has been less restricted and more privileged than elsewhere. Foreign observers are struck by the free expression permitted students in the United States and the relative informality of relations between students and teachers. Schools abroad tend to be more "authoritarian" and to operate, even at lowest levels, much more by lecture and rote recitation. At the same time, the adulthood of American youth is delayed by the prolongation of school years, the sheltered aspect of school life, and exclusion of youth from school and social power structures.

Student Movements Abroad

American government has been comparatively inactive in the affairs of youth, or the direct sponsorship of youth groups such as the Young Pioneers of the U.S.S.R. Perhaps the major efforts flowing from government initiative, aside from C.I.A. support, have been 4H clubs, the Peace Corps, and—in depression days—the Civilian Conservation Corps and National Youth Administration. Nor have political parties stimulated youth groups comparable to those in Israel, for example, where about 90 percent belong to politically oriented but autonomous youth groups engaging mainly in civic projects.

The Japanese student movement, Zengakuren (All Japan Federation of College Student Governments), began with the spreading labor movement after the second World War and the opposition to occupation efforts to decentralize Japanese higher education, admit girls, abolish national texts, and purge the militaristic curriculum. It is believed that communists took a leading part in its organization.[22] As it was suppressed it finally linked itself to off-campus political groups. In South Africa, the National Union of South African Students, a mass organization in English-speaking colleges, became for an extended period the strongest voice of opposition to official apartheid policy.

European post-war student movements rose mainly in protest against university traditions which in most places were still dominated by the medieval scholastic tradition. They also protested the conditions of student life. Beginning in the early 'sixties, student strikes over university and political issues were held throughout Italy, and were followed by French demonstrations over what students claimed were deplorable conditions at the Sorbonne and a curriculum laid down by seventeenth-century Jesuits.[23]

Student trade-unionsm spread from France to all of Western Europe. "This movement has been remarkable for its capacity to enlist wide and often heterogeneous support," Pinner says.[24] It recognizes as an expression of basic belief that "the student is a young intellectual worker." Among its demands are democratization of higher education, widening of the social base from which students are chosen, student salaries for academic work, participation in university administration, increased social services for students, modernization of curriculum, more contact with professors, fewer lectures, and more seminars. A mass movement, rather than a minority group, it was formerly dominated in France by Catholics and later by syndicalists.

Latin-American universities tend to be much older than those in the United States. When Harvard College was founded in 1636, Spain had already established twelve universities in Latin America, and some were almost 100

[22] Michiya Shimbori, "Comparisons Between Pre- and Post-War Student Movements in Japan," *Sociology of Education* (Fall, 1963), 37:62.

[23] D. C. Watt, "European Students Strike for Academic Reforms," *The Reporter* (December 16, 1965).

[24] Frank A. Pinner, "Student Trade-Unionism in France, Belgium and Holland," *Sociology of Education* (Spring, 1964), 37:3, 177.

18

years old. While some American universities responded to industrialization and the need for practical instruction, Latin-American universities tended to perpetuate archaic and aristocratic traditions. When university reform came to Latin America in the early twentieth century, the university was brought into closer touch with the outside world, and students demanded and got a voice in university affairs.[25]

Student protest in Latin America has been directed against university obsolescence, control of society by small elites, and the difficulties college graduates have in finding jobs in their professions. Student action appears to be, in many cases, a substitute for extra-curricular activities, absent in Latin-American universities, but present as a diversion to many American students. In Latin countries, where 65 to 70 percent of the population is under 30, students are taken seriously and given high social status. They have seats on almost all university governing councils, sometimes as many as one-third of the total.

In communist nations, student protest groups are rare, while government-sponsored youth groups, carrying on propaganda, service, and recreational functions, have flourished. One official Chinese view claims that the purpose of students of Mao is clear, "They are studying to revolutionize themselves ideologically." [26] When Chinese universities became, instead, the locus of dissent from government policy, they were closed in 1966 while the youthful "Red Guard" harassed the "deviationist" scholars. The U.S.S.R. youth organization, Komsomol, claims membership of 22 million.

Government youth services have sprung up in many nations, and many have become Ministries for Youth. Thus the out-of-school activity of youth has attained official status and become a government affair. The Yugoslav parliament reserves a number of seats for representatives of youth. In the mid-fifties, five percent of American youth had taken part in an organized youth movement at some time; in the United Kingdom the figure was 54 percent and in West Germany 30 percent.[27]

Schools of Education

Another major power bloc in higher learning is the school of education.[28] James Conant concludes that the establishment in higher education contains two hostile camps. "One camp is composed of professors of education allied with classroom teachers and public school administrators; . . . the other is composed of professors of the sciences and humanities and of influential collegiate alumni." [29] Within schools of education, he says, are many dissenters who are not allied with the educational establishment.

Much of the contention between liberal arts and education schools has its source in the expansion of schools of education (and other professional schools) and the decline of liberal arts schools and general education.[30] In 1963–64,

[25] David Nasatir, "Student Action in Latin America," *Transaction* (March–April, 1965).

[26] Hu Yao-Pang, "Revolutionize Our Youth," a pamphlet published without publication source, p. 34.

[27] UNESCO Study, *New Trends in Youth Organization*, No. 35 (1960).

[28] Forty-four percent of teacher education institutions are church connected; 18 percent are private non-church; and 38 percent are public.

[29] Conant, *The Education of American Teachers, op. cit.*, p. 7.

[30] While Jacques Barzun has claimed that the liberal arts are moribund, under a double attack from graduate schools that want specialists trained and high school advanced placement programs, Daniel Bell proposes reforms to revive liberal arts. His reforms offer a senior year course to relate liberal arts to modern problems and to the student's major. Daniel Bell, *The Reforming of General Education* (New York: Columbia University Press, 1965).

19

113,000 bachelors degrees were awarded in education, compared with 79,800 in all of the social sciences, including economics, history, political science, sociology, and the applied areas of public administration and social work. At the graduate level, 40,800 masters degrees were awarded in education and 9,500 in social sciences; 2,400 doctorates in education, and 1,800 in all the social sciences.

Successes of liberal arts schools within the university are seen in the inclination of some education schools (as Harvard, Chicago, Columbia) to surrender their undergraduate programs to liberal arts schools and concentrate on graduate education and internship training. The mounting demand for teacher training is likely to strengthen and expand schools of education, however, particularly as they adapt to criticism by improving instruction and hiring faculty from academic disciplines.

It is not certain what effect, if any, the outcome of this power struggle will have on the public schools since no evidence exists that one group is more effective than the other at preparing teachers. The competition between the two may help improve college instruction and shake up the "old" educational establishment.

power, II:
public schools

three

Powerful groups in the society are likely to have concurrent power in the schools, even though such power may lie dormant except when high-level decisions are made. This power is often hidden and invisible to the layman. For this reason, the protest of dissatisfied groups is usually aimed at teachers and other visible targets rather than at the organizers and managers of the system.

External Power

Critical decisions in the schools control the quantity, quality, and equality of education, for these are influenced by decisions about finance, stratification, and institutional flexibility. *Traditional*, or conservative, power groups have generally opposed federal financing of schools, the expansion of schools to include a broader population base, and institutional change which would lead to more democratic and egalitarian education. *Liberal* groups, often in coalition with *insurgents*, have favored federal aid, rapid institutional change, and movement toward a national, more equitable educational system.

Corporate Roles

The corporate groups that dominate the national economy and wield great influence in the political system have played a central role in the affairs of those institutions—colleges, universities, and others—that edu-

21

cate elites and train high-level personnel. Such corporate influence has offered status and direct financial rewards in the business world. These same groups, however, have generally been content to participate, from the sidelines, in a political coalition to preserve the *status quo* in public schools, assert states' rights in education, resist federal authority, and minimize school taxes on business and industry. Like all coalitions, this one has been unstable, and, as indicated before, significant parts of it seem to have reversed position on the schools in favor of national interests.

In the mid-nineteenth century business support of public education was mainly a response to recurrent unemployment of the period and trade union demands for universal free education. These demands, within limits, were not out of step with business interests—the need for an educated work force, the desire to absorb surplus and restless laborers, and the aim to socialize them to a middle-class way of life.

In general, it was assumed that educational institutions should operate in much the same way as business organizations and that their primary management function should be "efficiency" and especially the reduction of operating costs. The result of this view was to divert attention from education to cost saving and mechanical functions. As one advocate put it, "Our schools are, in a sense, factories in which the raw products are to be shaped and fashioned into products to meet the various demands of life." [1] Unfortunately, some of the more penurious and mechanical features of business activity were thus transferred to the schools.

Rarely have corporate leaders taken much direct interest in the management of local schools. Only in the suburbs where they reside have they played direct roles, as advisers or members of school boards. Businessmen's participation in schools is greatest when the dominant economic interest in the community is local and relatively small-scale. When corporate enterprise or more cosmopolitan groups are dominant, school involvements diminish. [2]

In towns and small cities, local small businessmen, however limited their perspective, have dominated the schools, as they have local affairs generally. [3] Their outlook has usually been "economy-minded" and constricting, except where building construction and other direct profit interests have been involved. They have favored reduced costs, elimination of "frills," emphasis on traditional behavior and practical studies, and development of personality rather than scholarship.

Public school boards have been composed almost exclusively of businessmen and professionals, and the values of the local school and its administrators have generally been those of middle-class, small-town, white Protestant America.

"External power agents," says Neal Gross, "frequently attempt to influence basic school decisions. . . ." [4] These external agents include economic groups (such as taxpayer's associations and the Chamber of Commerce), economically influential individuals (especially in small communities), local politicians, and religious groups. Local universities may also be represented in the power structure.

Both corporate and local groups have used the schools for business and

[1] Ellwood Cubberley, *Public School Administration* (Boston: Houghton Mifflin, 1916), pp. 337–338.
[2] Robert C. Schulze, "Economic Dominance in Community Power Structure," *American Sociological Review* (February, 1958), 23:3–9.
[3] C. Wright Mills and Melville J. Ulmer, *Small Business and Civic Welfare* (Washington: Government Printing Office, 1946).
[4] Neal Gross, "Who Controls the Schools?" *Educational and Public Policy* in Seymour Harris (ed.) (Berkeley, California: McCutchan, 1965), p. 26.

power, II: public schools

political purposes. It is claimed that the cost of free instructional material entering the nation's schools from private sources is greater than the cost of textbooks.[5] This material usually comes from business sources, including the National Association of Manufacturers and the Chamber of Commerce, and mixes education with argument in support of "free enterprise" and subtle product advertisement.[6] Other organizations, such as labor and ethnic groups, also contribute materials but they have been a negligible part of the total.

However limited their perspective, small businessmen have nonetheless been actively engaged in school affairs. The distress of big cities has resulted in large part from the relative absence of both cosmopolitian and local groups from school and community, creating a power vacuum into which new groups have begun to move.

Labor

Labor unions, when they are requested, says Gross, are major supporters of educational reform: "In my judgment this is one of the great untapped resources. Most school boards tend to have upper-class members, and it simply never occurs to them to talk with the unions. But the unions have great power which can be used for the benefit of the schools." [7]

Organized labor played a major role in agitation leading to the extension of education to lower-income groups and has engaged in partisan politics with enough success to influence some government education policies. It has had least influence, however, in state government, the level of greatest expansion and influence in education. Generally, state governments, because of the apportionment system, have been under the control of rural, traditional, and local small-business groups.

Stimulants to trade union involvement in school affairs have been: (1) the organization of teachers into trade unions; (2) increasing participation of labor in school board election and on local boards; and (3) federal awards to unions for training, poverty, and work-study programs.

Religious Groups

Religious controversy in the schools has been greatly diminished by legal compromise, the secularization of society, and the modernization of religious sects; and religious disputes have been dwarfed by racial and class conflict. Religious groups remain, however, a significant power in the total education system. About six million children are educated in private schools (about one in seven) and more than 90 percent of all private schools are Roman Catholic. In cities such as New York, Chicago, Pittsburgh, between 30 and 40 percent of children have been enrolled in private schools, and in some states enrollment has been as high as a quarter of all students.[8] As a result of an increased Catholic population and dissatisfaction of both Negroes and whites with urban schools, parochial schools grew 129 percent between 1940 and 1960 compared with a growth of 53 percent in public schools.

Parochial schools have tended to coexist rather than compete with public schools. Public awards to parochial schools have come almost exclusively from

[5] William O. Stanley, *Education and Social Integration* (New York: Columbia University Press, 1953), pp. 6–9.

[6] Two past presidents of the NAM have served on the Advisory Council of the John Birch Society, a group that greatly increased its political activities in schools during the 1960's.

[7] Gross, *op. cit.*, p. 35.

[8] Nonpublic school enrollment as a percentage of total enrollment in elementary and secondary schools in 1959–1960 include: California 9.8; Georgia 3.0; Indiana 11.3; Massachusetts 22.2; New York 22.6; North Carolina 1.4; Wisconsin 25.8.

Table 1

Individuals or Groups Who Exert Pressure *	Percentage of Superintendents Reporting Pressure, N-105
Parents or PTA	92
Individual school board members	75
Teachers	65
Taxpayers' association	49
Town finance committee	48
City Council politicians	46
Business or commercial organizations	45
Individuals influential for economic reasons	44
Personal friends	37
The press	36
Old-line families	30
Church or religious groups	28
Veterans organizations	27
Labor unions	27
Chamber of Commerce	23
Service clubs	20
Fraternal organizations	13
Farm organizations	12
Welfare organizations	3

* Neal Gross, *Who Runs Our Schools?* (New York: Wiley, 1958), p. 50.

federal funds since non-Protestant influence is greatest at that level.[9] Such funds have taken the form of grants for noninstructional purposes, aid for joint facilities with the public schools (as supplementary educational centers), and, in higher education, stipends to students (as the G.I. Bill).

Other Groups

Parent and other organizations that impinge on the schools are, with some minor but growing exceptions, middle class. Gross reports on the percentage of superintendents who said they were exposed to pressures from specified individuals and groups. These superintendents tended to think, though, that citizens' apathy rather than pressure was their main problem.

Internal Power: The Old Establishment

The National Education Association

Because of decentralization and lack of coordination in education, voluntary associations abound. These include 500 regional and national associations of education, nearly 150 college professional societies, 50 religious educational associations, and 15 international educational associations, or a total of about 1,100 private associations. The organization that clearly dominates all others is the National Education Association, its power stemming from a deficit of federal authority. The NEA is neither an official public organization nor a representative private body, yet its influence has exceeded that of any other group, including the U.S. Office of Education, state departments of education, and local school boards.

[9] The Roman Catholic Church operates a national organization which is the equivalent of the National Education Association, and its headquarters are, like the NEA's, in Washington, D. C.; it also operates the National Catholic Welfare Conference, a large national organization with departments in education, youth, social action, and so on.

power, II: public schools

The principal critics of the NEA and the "educational establishment" have been university officials and unionized teachers. According to James B. Conant, the most influential among the university spokesmen, the educational establishment consists of the NEA, school administrators, accrediting associations, and teacher-training institutions. This establishment, he asserts, is dominated by school administrators through the NEA. "It seems clear that any amorphous unofficial body composed of public school administrators and professors of education is not now well suited to establishing policy for our public schools." [10]

In another statement, Conant included in the establishment: state departments of education, some classroom teachers, professors of education, and the executive staffs of organizations such as the School Boards Association and the PTA. ". . . Any powerful new group that begins to make itself heard on educational matters can expect overtures from the establishment." [11] He advocates that state departments of education be strengthened as a countervailing power, despite his assertion that they are already part of the establishment.

The NEA claims a membership of over 940,000 and employs over 900 people at its spacious Washington, D.C. headquarters.[12] Its influence extends directly into all educational activity including the certification of teachers, the accreditation of teacher-training institutions, and dominance of the World Confederation of Organizations of the Teaching Professions (WCOTP).[13]

In the past, NEA alliances with groups such as the American Legion and the AMA have been close. In 1921 a joint committee was established to promote cooperation with the Legion, and since then Legion speakers have appeared regularly on NEA programs. The two groups continue their cooperative committee, their sponsorship of American Education Week, and their joint efforts to promote "patriotism and citizenship," [14] as they see it.

Close liaison has existed throughout NEA history with traditional groups, though many individual officers and members have been political liberals. In the early days of labor organizations, for example, the NEA supported employers and opposed strikes. In 1877 when labor was organizing, the NEA president declared that the schools should teach respect for organized industry and private property. For a long period after the Supreme Court decision on desegregation, the NEA retained segregated Southern chapters and delayed taking a strong position against school segregation and educational inequality.

Like other large and enduring organizations, the NEA has learned to adapt to change, absorb opponents, and abruptly alter policy when necessary. The most serious challenge to it has come from the American Federation of Teachers, a trade union engaged in collective bargaining and direct action. Faced with this competition, the NEA changed its venerable tradition of peaceful accommodation and engaged in similar action.

The effect of the NEA hegemony has been, said Conant, to do away

[10] James B. Conant, *The Education of American Teachers* (New York: McGraw-Hill, 1965), p. 8.

[11] *Ibid.*

[12] In one recent year, the NEA published 20 monthly magazines, 181 bulletins, 36 yearbooks and other books, and 1,070 miscellaneous materials, and it has been the nation's largest education research center.

[13] Several international federations of teachers exist including: (1) the WCOTP, dominated by the West and the NEA; (2) the IFFTU (Interntaional Federation of Free Teachers Unions), a trade union federation with which the AFT is associated; (3) World Federation of Teachers' Union with headquarters in Prague and membership drawn largely from communist groups.

[14] Edgar B. Wesley, *NEA: The First Hundred Years* (New York: Harper, 1957).

with foreign language instruction in the schools between 1930 and 1950, ignore Negro education, and through its control of state authorities, to divert teacher training from the main stream of higher education.

Perhaps the most positive function of the NEA has been to give education national status. Through it, the diverse threads of education were tied together and given more strength than they might otherwise have had. Some critics say that the real effect of NEA national operations, concerned as they were with state groups, and reflecting a rather traditional view of government function, was to delay the involvement of the federal government in public schools. "If asked what the NEA has accomplished during the past century on behalf of the primary and secondary schools," said Francis Keppel while U.S. Commissioner of Education, "one would have to reply, 'Not much.'"

Officially, the NEA supported federal aid to schools but, said Keppel, ". . . it has often taken the position that, in effect, 'we need the money, but we oppose Federal direction of how to spend it.'" The NEA's "success in this matter has created a barrier to Federal aid. There is an inherent conflict between desire for freedom from legislative limitations and desire for Federal appropriations." [15]

NEA officials, like other public school officials, appear to be predominantly white Anglo-Saxon Protestant, with attitudes reflecting those of the small-town business and minor-professional community.

Administrators

In the schools, as in most organizations, the professional managers tend to dominate the organization. Their authority varies in each organization, but they are never fully independent of the overseers who hire and fire them, pay them, and review their work. The overseer of the school administrator is the local board of education. This board though possessing legal authority is usually unpaid, part-time, and highly transient. In practice, therefore, the "bureaucracy" of administrators (superintendents, principals, and so on), by virtue of numbers, permanence in office, and full-time status often has far greater operating power than their governing boards. [16] The imbalance may be seen in New York City, for example, where the Board of Education consists of nine people, all serving part-time, while the bureaucracy of full-time administrators, number about 5,500. Unless the nine citizens are unusually able and active, they cannot begin to control the bureaucracy's behavior, nor can the superintendent they hire to direct the bureaucracy. In New York City and other places the superintendent has no power to appoint his own staff but must take only those who come from the ranks and who are seasoned in the system. The New York City system includes a headquarters staff of 3,000, an operational staff of 2,200 principals and assistant principals, 31 district superintendents, and 740 department chairmen. A core supervisory group, according to Marilyn Gittell, includes some 30 headquarters staff, the Board of Examiners (who in effect "hire" and promote teachers and administrators), 20 or 30 assistant superintendents, and a few active directors of special bureaus—all but two of the

---

[15] Francis Keppel, "Education Lobbies and Federal Legislation," *Challenge and Change in American Education*, Seymour Harris, ed. (Berkeley, California: McCutchon, 1965), p. 66.

[16] Even the Roman Catholic church, assumed to be controlled by Papal authority, has its own powerful bureaucracy. "Until the Council started in Rome," writes Cartus, "the nature and even the existence of the Vatican bureaucracy was unknown. . . . The Curia is a tightly knit organization . . . of not more than a dozen men who . . . maintain an absolute stranglehold on every decision made by any department of the organization."

group bred within the city system. The strongest of the group are the 30 at headquarters.[17]

In the United States, about 10 percent of education staff is engaged full time in administration, and it is estimated that in the schools of New York state more administrators are employed than in all of Western Europe.

Because they usually have tenure, school administrators cannot easily be discharged. Only the superintendent works on a time contract and is relatively mobile. Unlike business executives, school administrators below the level of superintendent seldom change employers or move to other systems. Moreover, formidable barriers to "outsiders" are erected, making the systems even more ingrown and immobile. Unless the superintendent in a large system is drawn from inside the system, he is often faced with a bitter power struggle within the organization. School boards may try to introduce "new blood" into the system by hiring younger men from other systems, but these newcomers may be undercut in their efforts to innovate by a core of experienced and resistant administrators.

Administrators make the rules and set the tone for the school. "It is becoming a cliché," says school administrator Carl Marburger, "that the local school administrator is the most significant individual in the lives of children and youth." The degree to which a school is open or closed, he claims, "is determined by the style of administration," and the most obvious deterrent to enthusiastic and imaginative teaching—the key to learning—is, for example, "the authoritarian who sees his school as an armed camp." [18] The superintendent is the system's power center. He can often be compared with industrial executives in the size of his organization and the salary he earns.[19]

CHARACTERISTICS. Little is known about school administrators. "Very little research has been done, and few school systems use formal evaluation systems for principals, or other administrators." [20] According to a national survey, more than 40 percent of school principals had businessmen fathers, and another 15 percent were sons of farmers. More than 10 percent were sons of professionals, and about 20 percent had fathers who were skilled and unskilled blue-collar workers. More than 50 percent had fathers with only a grade school education, and only about 10 percent of the fathers had been to college. Administrators within a system often belong to the same social group, such as the Rotary, American Legion, or similar groups with large memberships of small businessmen. Because many are from business and few from professional backgrounds, administrators may concern themselves more with business and administrative duties than instructional matters in the school.

"They are in their late fifties and early sixties," says Gross about administrators. ". . . It takes a long time to get up there. And when you talk with these men, you get a curious feeling of inertia. You throw out an idea and the reaction is 'It can't be done' or 'Oh, we heard about that years ago.' The man

[17] Marilyn Gittell, *Participants and Participation* (New York: Center for Urban Education, 1966).

[18] Carl L. Marburger, *The Disadvantaged*, Mott Institute for Community Improvement, College of Education, Michigan State University (April, 1966), 1:2, 1.

[19] The Chicago school superintendent has, for example, been among the highest-paid public officials. His salary of $48,500 in the mid-sixties was topped only by that of the President of the United States and the governor and mayor of New York.

[20] J. K. Hemphill, D. E. Griffiths, and N. Frederiksen, *Administrative Performance and Personality* (New York: Columbia University Press, 1962), p. 348.

27

on top may want to make changes in the schools but he has to work through this structure and it may be very difficult." [21]

At one end of a personality continuum is the rigidly authoritarian administrator, and on the other, the man who simply echoes the last opinion he heard. If a school superintendent has been in trouble, Gross observes, "he has the stigma. He is through. That is why so many school superintendents are, more or less, double talkers. You listen, and you are not sure what they are saying, because they have learned to cover their words with a certain protective coating." He adds that some are "major heroes, in my judgement, fighting a real battle for public education. I don't see how they take it." [22]

POWER DISTRIBUTION. Many superintendents are distressed by the "interference" of lay citizen groups and school boards. "Because teaching, supervision, and administration have been specialized professions," says an administrator publication, "the modern board of education cannot waste its time and jeopardize educational results by trying to do the work of technically trained educators." [23] Gross reports that one out of five superintendents interviewed said their school boards constituted a "major obstacle to their carrying out their jobs in a professional manner." [24]

School administration is a decidedly hierarchical and disciplined business and the top administrator, the local school superintendent, holds the key position in each school district. Indeed, there seems to be professional agreement that the most significant duty of the people's representatives on the local school board is the selection of the superintendent. [25]

Though debate continues about "democratic" administration, available evidence suggests the desirability of greater power sharing within school systems. Griffiths, for example, found that, in school systems where there was greater staff participation in decision-making, the superintendent was rated "most successful" in the performance of his duties. [26]

Since many groups have been demanding and getting a share of school power, the future will very likely witness a greater distribution of authority to teachers, citizens, students, and individual schools. [27] At the same time, a contrasting tendency to centralize certain other powers in the hands of a national authority is likely.

Power may also be shared among administrators. Many school principals now "have surprisingly little control over what is to be taught and by whom. Largely excluded from policy making, they tend to behave like feudal barons whose grudging cooperation the superintendent must constantly woo." [28]

In many systems the lines of authority have become so obscure to the public that buck-passing between principals and higher administration prevents decision-making and change.

21 Gross, "Who Controls the Schools?", *op. cit.*, p. 33.
22 *Ibid.*, p. 25.
23 *School Boards in Action* (Washington, D. C.: American Association of School Administrators, 1946), p. 11.
24 Gross, "Who Controls the Schools?", *op. cit.*, p. 26.
25 Thomas H. Eliot, "Toward an Understanding of Public School Politics," *American Political Science Review* (December, 1959), 53:1032–1051.
26 D. E. Griffiths, *An Evaluation of the Leadership of the School Superintendent,* unpublished Yale University doctoral dissertation, 1952.
27 Most organizations, including the military, have been under pressure to relax central authority.
28 Allan R. Talbot, "Needed: A New Breed of School Superintendent," *Harper's Magazine* (February, 1966), 81–87.

RECRUITMENT. Administrators, even more than teachers, are recruited from a narrow group of eligibles. In most places, the superintendent is required to have at least six years of college and teaching experience as well as many specific courses in education and school administration. Conant has proposed that superintendents be chosen, as are college presidents and corporation executives, without regard to formal credentials or course credits. A nationwide talent hunt for leaders in all walks of life who would receive university and apprenticeship training for school leadership has also been suggested.

The exclusion of women from administrative posts has seriously narrowed the range of eligibles. Very likely some of the richest talent resources can be found among women teachers who compose about three-fourths of the profession. In a study of principals, both teachers and administrators rated women principals higher than males on performance, knowledge of teaching methods, and democratic behavior.[29] Although men are only 7 percent of elementary school teachers, they make up 59 percent of elementary principals.

School Boards

Schools have been outside the popular political structure of the nation, financially autonomous, and supervised usually by nonpartisan local boards chosen in separate elections.[30] Removal from popular and partisan contest has made schools less accessible to lower-income groups who tend to vote only in partisan elections, and has detached them from the two-party system of American politics. Popular participation in the affairs of school boards is so limited that two-thirds of boards report they usually have fewer than five outsiders attending meetings, and most boards meet only once a month for two hours. About 40 percent of boards do not open their meetings to the public. Even in cities (where low-income groups hold some political power) the number of citizen representatives on school boards is so small and the school system and its bureaucracy so vast that these citizens have little effective control.

Local school board members number about 200,000 (or about one for every nine teachers). Two-thirds are businessmen and farmers, and in ethnic background they are overwhelmingly white Anglo-Saxon Protestant. Their average age is about 47. In the largest school districts, those enrolling more than 25,000 students, 75 percent of board members are businessmen or professionals.[31] Manual workers, including the skilled, total only 8.5 percent and only 2.4 percent in large urban districts. Nearly half are college graduates and only one in ten does not have a high school diploma. North Carolina law requires that a board member be a "man of good business qualifications," and other states have required board members to own property assessed for school taxes.[32]

Fewer than one of ten board members are women. More than half of the boards have no women members at all, and of the other half, only 12 percent had more than one woman member. W. W. Charters suggests that the

[29] Hemphill, et al., op. cit.
[30] About 95 percent of school boards are elected. In 32 states, school elections are nonpartisan. In 1950 about 60 percent of systems were fiscally independent.
[31] Roy M. Caughran, "The School Board Member Today," American School Board Journal (November, 1956), 133:39 and (December, 1956), 26.
[32] The largest proportion of board members, 35 percent, are businessmen; professional and technical 27 percent, farmers 12 percent, housewives 7 percent, clerks and skilled workers 6 percent. Report of the National School Boards Association, 1965.

social-class position of board members does not influence their vote on educational issues. But since boards have been composed so exclusively of middle- and upper-income members, it is difficult to predict what boards composed of manual workers, lower-income groups, or their representatives would do with such power.[33]

State Boards of Education

State boards of education perhaps derive greatest authority from the fact that they often control the state colleges of education and the certification of teachers.[34] Their control of certification enables them to decide what candidates must do in order to become certified teachers. Thus, they control the supply of teachers, the kind of training these teachers receive, and the curriculum and influence of teacher training institutions.

Teachers, however, want to control their own certification in order to control professional standards, raise teacher salaries by limiting entry of new teachers, and exercise influence over teacher training and schools of education. Myron Lieberman, a spokesman of the AFT and organized teachers, says, "The NEA deplores low standards for teaching. In fact, the standards are low because teachers have no control over them, and they have no control over these standards because the NEA does not believe in it. Since 1921 at least, the NEA has advocated non-professional control of the state boards. . . . The really ominous fact is that in a growing number of states, teachers are excluded *by law* from the boards which control entry to teaching." [35] In contrast, lawyers, physicians, dentists, accountants, real estate brokers, and many others establish and administer the standards to be met in almost all states by aspirants for admission to their profession. Conant wishes to strengthen the state board's position vis-à-vis NEA and change certification requirements to reduce the importance of training received in schools of education.

Parent Organizations

The PTA is the largest of the parent organizations, with a membership of 12 million in 1960, or six times its 1940 membership. It is generally acknowledged to be a traditional group that has, in most systems, been greatly influenced by school administrators.[36] Its stronghold is the small town and suburb. In general, the more remote the community the more active the PTA. The organization, says William Kvaraceus, "should change its name to the Parent-Principal Association." [37] PTA policy, he points out, favors the NEA and finds the AFT distasteful. "Since the first PTA chairman rapped the first gavel, the PTA has been run as a closed middle-class shop." Even when the PTA leadership, "so unimaginative, tradition-bound and timid, grows momentarily bold, the local units lie low. For example, the PTA's National Congress did venture to take a stand on federal aid to education legislation. (They were for it.) But many locals didn't dare put the issue to a vote."

---

[33] W. W. Charters, Jr., "Social Class Analysis and Control of Public Education," *Harvard Educational Review* (Fall, 1953), 23:268–283.

[34] A few state education offices have large and permanent bureaucracies. The New York department, for example, is larger than the U.S. Office of Education, employing 2,350 persons at administrative levels alone.

[35] Myron Lieberman, *The Future of Public Education* (Chicago: University of Chicago Press, 1960), pp. 184–85.

[36] Gresham Sykes, "The PTA and Parent-Teacher Conflict," *Harvard Educational Review* (Spring, 1953), 23:2, 86–92.

[37] William C. Kvaraceus, "The PTA is a Waste of Time," *Saturday Evening Post* (May 2, 1964), 6.

Parent groups are in many places a significant and influential part of the educational establishment. Almost all of the permanent and powerful groups have been white and middle-class, even in the cities. Negroes and other disadvantaged minorities have formed neighborhood groups in many places but in no cases have they matched in size, resources, and influence the competing middle-class organizations. In New York City, David Rogers claims, school desegregation was effectively blocked by an alliance of some school officials, real estate interests, and two powerful respected and moderate white citizen groups. He looks to intervention from the mayor, the state board of education, and the federal government to overcome this alliance.[38]

Insurgents and New Establishments

Unionized Teachers

The most militant assertion of teacher interests has been led by the AFT, a trade union affiliate of the AFL-CIO. Its growth from 46,600 members in 1955 to about 135,000 in 1966 was accelerated by the political power of labor in the cities where it has most of its membership.[39]

The AFT has insisted that teachers become education policy makers. "The most important causes of the ineffectiveness of public education," says Lieberman, "are rooted in its anachronistic and dysfunctional power structure. Because most current controversy is concerned with the rightness or wrongness of certain educational policies and not with the power structure within which these policies are made, it is largely irrelevant to the basic problems of education."[40]

The AFT wishes to raise standards from what Mortimer Kreuter calls the "brown paper bag way of thinking." Teachers "talk and act 'poor mouth,'" he says, "bringing their lunches to school in brown paper bags, eating in the same rooms with their pupils or in a grimy teachers' lounge. Teachers are graded and inspected very much like children. . . . They literally have no time to go to the toilet. . . . They must punch time clocks twice daily and file affidavits when ill. . . . In our efforts to bring innovations and creativity into the teaching professions, we must first come to grips with the teacher's infantilization at the hands of the system."[41]

Teachers should develop, says Lieberman, a strong national organization rather than trying to build local citizens' committees. "A person who has a position of authority in the U.S. Chamber of Commerce can do more to help public education by modifying some of the educational policies of this organization than thousands of citizens could accomplish by breathing down the necks of their school boards once a month."[42] He urges that teachers become political: ". . . The work of teachers is dominated by political considerations but the teachers themselves are political nonentities. The need is to transform teachers into political animals. . . . Without political power, teachers will

[38] David Rogers, *Obstacles to School Desegregation in New York City: A Benchmark Case* (New York: Center for Urban Education, 1966), mimeographed.

[39] During 1965–66, about half of AFT members were in five cities, and exclusive bargaining rights had been won in New York, Chicago, Philadelphia, Detroit, and other cities.

[40] Lieberman, *op. cit.*, p. 5.

[41] Mortimer Kreuter, "The Teacher in the Brown Paper Bag," *The Urban Review* (May, 1966), 272.

[42] Lieberman, *op. cit.*, p. 272.

31

never be able to protect the integrity of their work." [43] Teachers in general have been characterized by political conservatism and neutrality, although city teachers are more liberal and politically active than their community, according to Ziegler, while small-town teachers are more conservative.[44]

The most important problem in teacher education, Lieberman feels, is to decide *who* should determine its content and duration. He believes that teachers should make such decisions and asserts that "every major weakness of public education has its roots in higher education, and especially in the liberal arts colleges," where 80 percent of the education of teachers is now carried on. "For example, overemphasis upon athletics, social graces and 'adjustment,' the favorite whipping boys of our contemporary custodians of culture, are strictly hand-me-downs from the liberal arts colleges." [45] He favors high standards for teacher certification and use of aides to alleviate teacher shortages. Though his opinion may not represent general sentiment, he also favors merger of AFT and NEA to give teachers national power.

The Insurgent Poor

Groups external to the schools—notably those concerned with civil rights, poverty, and to some extent organized labor—have entered the political and educational scene in agitational and insurgent roles. Educators have made some accommodations to these groups by co-opting individual representatives rather than including their organizations in the permanent power structure.

Demands of civil rights groups for improved pupil performance, equality of opportunity, and desegregation have been most effective at the federal level. They have resulted in massive federal aid, the creation of community and education-related programs, and the establishment of the principle of "maximum feasible participation" of the poor in decision-making. The new power of these groups derives in large measure from political influence acquired as a result of Negro migration into Northern cities, but also from the assertion of voting rights in the South.

Powerless and alienated lower socioeconomic groups have sometimes voted against school bond issues out of negative feelings about the power structure of their towns and schools.[46] Social action and organization have created new interests among these groups in school affairs and have had an apparent influence on their self-image, sense of potency, and education aspiration.

According to Dan Dodson, the major function of the schools has been "to take all the children of the community and teach them their place in the power order." [47] They are taught in such a way that "all will understand their failures are their own, rather than those of the system. Otherwise they would rebel and blow the system apart." The alternative to the common approach of siphoning off the talented among the disadvantaged and alienating them from their group, he suggests, is for the powerless to take power and to "learn

[43] *Ibid.*, p. 285.

[44] Harmon Ziegler, *The Political World of the High School Teacher* (Eugene, Oregon: Center for the Advanced Study of Educational Administration, University of Oregon, 1966).

[45] *Ibid.*, p. 136.

[46] John E. Horton and Wayne E. Thompson, "Powerlessness and Political Negativism: A Study of Defeated Local Referendums," *The American Journal of Sociology* (March, 1962), 67:5, 485–493. (Interviews with about 400 voters in two upstate N. Y. communities in 1957 and 1958.)

[47] Dan W. Dodson, "Education and the Powerless," mimeographed speech, N.Y.U. Educational Sociology.

what the schools have to offer because they need it to prepare themselves to make their maximum contribution to the group's efforts. This approach calls for conflict . . . ."[48]

The Academy

Civil rights agitation, new funds, and the expansion of schools of education have aroused parts of the academic community to a new interest in the schools.

"When social changes in this century transformed the nature of the high school," said James B. Conant, "the typical college professor himself was viewing with disgust and dismay what was happening in the schools. With few exceptions, college professors turned their backs on the problem of mass secondary education and eyed with envy Great Britain and the Continent where such problems did not exist."[49]

"The 'Conant Establishment,'" said AFT President Charles Cogen, "a much more shadowy structure than the 'Educational Establishment,' might be considered to be a group of (largely nonpublic) university, college and foundation executives, along with some state education department officials who feel themselves restricted by the educational associations. Dr. Conant functions in a world of educational policy in which teachers have no part."[50]

In *Slums and Suburbs*, Conant was among the first to support greater equality of educational opportunity, an issue largely ignored by the "old" educational establishment. He has commended the "old" establishment for its record of "emphasis on education for citizenship, on the socially unifying effects of the comprehensive high school, and on the public school as instruments of democracy, the recognition of individual differences, and of the need for including practical courses in high school elective programs," but criticizes as does John W. Gardner, their neglect of "academic excellence."[51] A "new" establishment of academicians from higher education has risen to challenge the authority of the older school-administrator establishment.

Private and Public Initiatives

In the history of education, significant ideas and innovations originated mainly among nonschoolmen—Rousseau, Frobel, Mann, Herbart, James, Dewey, Thorndike, Montessori. Even the exceptions, Martin Mayer points out—Pestalozzi, Thring, Parker, Pankhurst—were pariahs in their own community and exerted influence mostly through articulate outsiders.[52]

Educational reform seems to emanate largely from the society—historical movements, technological developments, and power arrangements—rather than from the work of individuals, either in or outside of the educational system, though such social conditions may stimulate the work of inventors and innovators.

---

[48] *Ibid.*
[49] Conant, *op. cit.*, p. 5.
[50] Charles Cogen, "The Urgent Need for Planning in Education," *American Federationist* (March, 1965).
[51] John W. Gardner, *Excellence, Can We Be Equal and Excellent Too?* (New York: Harper, 1961).
[52] Martin Mayer, *Social Studies in American Schools* (New York: Harper Colophon Books, 1962).

Private Enterprises

A rather large-scale entry of business—big and small —into education marked the postwar years, coming in several forms:

1. *Philanthropic foundations and funds, financed by business and wealthy donors and controlled indirectly by these funding sources.* In 1960 there were about 15,000 private philanthropic foundations, with assets of about $12 billion; about 54 percent of their grants went to education. While these sources have invested principally in traditional and conservative programs—often in higher education—which benefit the business community, they have also moved into some more experimental education and social action projects.

2. *Profit and nonprofit enterprise.* Large corporations have moved for the first time into the "education industry" on a profit or nonprofit "cost" basis to: (a) package and sell books, programs, computers, talking typewriters, TV packages, audio-visual materials, language laboratories, etc., (b) conduct total training programs (job corps, work-study programs, etc.), (c) sell consultation and service ("know how" about conducting programs, making grant applications, lobbying, etc.), (d) carry on basic research and program evaluation. Perhaps the heaviest experimental investments—with predictions of the largest "payoff"—have been in computer instruction and retrieval technology.

Collectively, these enterprises—because many are powerful organizations with strong profit-making drives—are likely to make a profound impression on American education, for good and ill. They may help solve the technological and organizational problems of education as they have in industry, or they may simply sell expensive and useless equipment to educators. The policies, operations, and influence of these groups have not yet been documented.[53]

Federal Authorities

From the point of view of power, obviously the greatest of all organizations is the state, not only because it is the sole repository of the power of physical coercion, but it can call on resources of the whole community and has final regulative power over everything.[54]

The greatest point of stress in American education, as in politics, has been the role of the federal government. The traditional view has opposed federal activity, and the liberal-insurgent view has favored it.

Dwight Eisenhower, as president of Columbia University, wrote in 1949 that federal aid to education is "another vehicle by which the believers in paternalism, if not outright socialism, will gain still additional power for the central government." [55] As testimony to the flexibility of views and institutions, Eisenhower, as President of the United States, proposed large-scale school aid legislation and ended his term in office with warnings, not about expansion of federal power, but about the untamed power of the military-industrial complex.

[53] Among the independent "intellectual" centers of the nation, influencing social and educational policy are: The RAND Corporation, the Foreign Policy Association, The Carnegie Foundation, the Rockefeller Foundation, the Ford Foundation, the Center for the Study of Democratic Institutions, the Institute for Policy Studies, the Brookings Institution, the Russell Sage Foundation, the Committee for Economic Development, the Conference on Economic Progress, the Upjohn Institute for Employment Research, the American Assembly.

[54] Robert MacIver, *Power Transformed* (New York: Macmillan, 1964), p. 80.

[55] *Congressional Record* (June 14, 1949), 95:14, A369

The view that local control of schools has brought education closer to the people is disputed by Myron Lieberman: "This folklore persists in the face of the strongest kinds of evidence to refute it." Centralization of public education, "in whatever form it comes, will bring public education into the mainstream of American life." [56]

The first general federal aid programs passed by Congress in the mid-sixties resulted from the ascendancy of political liberalism in national politics. The functions of such aid were to accommodate the rising demands and expectations of the disadvantaged, and to promote national security and economic development through educational investments. Before that, most federal aid to education was defense-related and had gone primarily to higher education where the contribution to the economy seemed more direct and federal aid less debatable. Federal funds have also gone to vocational education, job training, and other economy-related programs. Federal civil rights legislation provided a national achievement testing program for the first time and concerned itself with educational equality and desegregation.

One of the most significant federal aid programs, the Morrill Act, was sponsored by the Republican Party and signed into law by Lincoln in 1862 after earlier opposition by Democratic President Buchanan. The network of colleges and universities established in all states under the Act revolutionized American higher education by bringing college within popular reach, especially in rural areas. Through agricultural experimental stations and cooperative extension services carried on by colleges, knowledge was made available to farmers and probably did much more to spur agricultural development and farm efficiency than any other factor.

In recent years the growth of federal aid to higher education for research and development has been phenomenal and now constitutes 75 percent of all federal assistance to higher education.[57]

The rigidity of the educational establishment has resulted in the creation, with federal aid, of educational institutions and programs that are competitive with the schools. As a response to the great depression of the 'thirties, the federal National Youth Administration was created, a youth organization that began to set up its own schools until its activities were terminated by the war.

Conant maintains that, "we can dismiss any talk of the federal government establishing and operating a federal system of schools or even a single school or college or university in one of the fifty sovereign states. Clearly a government without the power to establish educational institutions is hardly in a position to establish educational policy." [58] Instead, he proposed a compact for the creation of a Commission to formulate national education policy. This Commission, a legal agreement entered into by state legislatures, would bring together from the separate states, educators and public leaders to study problems, establish states' rights in education, decide national policy, and make recommendations to the states.[59]

"What weakens the argument about federal interference with local and

[56] Lieberman, *op. cit.*, pp. 284–85.

[57] In 1957–58, $534.4 million went to R and D, of which $368.9 million went to the top ten institutions. In 1947–48 only $95.3 million went to R and D in higher education. Direct federal aid to higher education amounted to $712.4 million in 1958.

[58] Conant, *Shaping Educational Policy, op. cit.*, p. 46.

[59] The Education of Commission of the States, with headquarters in Denver, is composed of voluntary membership of delegates from each state (the governor, 2 state legislators, and 4 citizens chosen by the governor). The Commission is expected to provide an alternative to present control of schools by administrators or the federal government. It strengthens the influence of higher education and state political leaders.

state policy is the past history of lack of effective state and local policy," says Fred Hechinger.[60] "For example, the money contributed by the NDEA of 1958 undoubtedly was welcome, but it is hard to believe that the local schools could not have got going on reform of mathematics, science and foreign language training long before the Federal Government took them by the hand. But the most persuasive case against the new anti-Washington voices is made—despite some shining personal exceptions—by the school administrator's role in racial segregation." While many innovative people have been introduced to the U.S. Office of Education and the anti-poverty program, for the most part, he says, school administrators are "conservative men, who see change, including change in educational goals and methods, as a threat."

Partisan Politics

Both the educational and the Conant establishments have strongly favored the removal of the schools from "partisan politics." The main objection to an elected chief state school officer, says Conant, is that "discussion of educational issues in a political campaign easily become emotional and irrational." [61]

Yet "politics" is the democratic means through which popular sentiments are expressed, and political *parties* are the vehicles for expression of programmatic and power interests. Removal of the school from politics appears to have diverted it from the main stream of national life, made it less amenable to change, and rendered it less responsive to the interests of lower socioeconomic groups.

Administrators tend to oppose even present political ties to nonpartisan school boards. Many claim, in effect, that "the schools are the special province of the professionals . . . the voters being a necessary evil who must be reckoned with because they provide the money." [62] Like most bureaucracies, they would like to run their own organization, without outside interference or public controls.

[60] Fred M. Hechinger, "Educators Still Balk at U.S. Role," *New York Times* (February 20, 1966).
[61] Conant, *Shaping Educational Policy, op. cit.,* p. 36.
[62] Thomas H. Eliot, *op. cit.,* pp. 53, 1032–1051.

the economy:
control centers
four

Both general sociology and the sociology of education have had a close kinship with economics, though they have not always been on speaking terms. Sociology was first taught in university economics departments, and many early sociologists were partisans of economic ideologies. William Graham Sumner, perhaps America's first sociologist, offered the Darwinian principles of natural selection as a rationale for the fiercest exploitation of early capitalism. Lester Ward, on the other side, was an advocate of egalitarian reform in school and society. Burned on conflict over social Darwinism, Marxism, and other ideologies, sociologists and educators have moved ever closer to empirical psychology, with a recent tendency to circle back again to economic analysis.

Similarly, economics has usually entered considerations of the school only as an ideological issue, though more recently it has been used in other ways. Any consideration of school and society must give a high priority to the economic system and its influence on virtually everything that occurs in the society.[1] Perhaps the most serious oversight of those who would solve social problems relating to the schools, social services, control of deviance, and so forth, is their inattention to economic growth, manpower needs, distribution of wealth, investment priorities, and other economic factors.

[1] The highest priority in many societies is held by the military and defense system which has an, as yet, undefined relationship to the educational system.

37

The Three Systems

In the United States, the political and economic systems are separate—one publicly and the other privately controlled—and the schools are largely outside both systems. In the U.S.S.R., the political, economic, and educational systems are *in*separable and are governed by one bureaucracy, the Communist Party. As a result, schools in the U.S.S.R. are more likely to be used by the political system for propaganda purposes and by the economic system for manpower-training purposes. The relative fiscal and administrative autonomy of American schools have made them relatively marginal to both systems. The advantages to separation are greater autonomy and stability during periods of rapid power shifts; the disadvantages, a tendency to be out of synchronization with the larger systems and their changing needs. Governing bureaucracies in monolithic societies may make long-term economic plans, for example, and correspondingly expand education to meet the manpower training needs of economic expansion.

The Needs of Economic Systems

Economic systems interact with educational systems in various ways. Feudal economies required literacy and formal education only for a small elite: landowners, clerics, some merchants and artisans. The manpower needs of industrial systems required large numbers of skilled and literate workers and, despite the warnings of some eighteenth-century economists against government intiatives, public education was extended. Without mass literacy and job skills modern industry would not have been possible.

Economic theories have their counterparts in the school. Between the extremes of *laissez faire* and socialist eocncmic theories, Keynesian economics asserted that government should stimulate and stabilize the privately owned economy through fiscal, monetary, and employment policies. In the United States, government has begun to operate essentially on these Keynesian principles, performing through the "New Economics," a thermostatic function for the economy. The trend toward more and new types of public intervention has its effects in the schools. Early colonial schools were privately operated. When public schools were established they were in most cases fiscally independent of other government levels. When the local school tax was no longer adequate, state governments intervened, and most recently the federal government has taken over where the state left off, providing new forms of aid, stimulation, and regulation to the schools.

Growth

Economic growth rates affect the whole society—jobs, prosperity, opportunity, and funds available for schools. Growth rates have been the subject of much political conflict. Many traditional groups have favored restraint, increased interest rates, decreased government spending, and wage controls, while most liberals have favored high growth rates to reduce unemployment and raise the general standard of living.

Rapid growth increases the power of lower income groups by raising their expectations and wage bargaining power, and by urbanizing, educating, and organizing them. Growth stimulates the public appetite for education, increases opportunities in skilled and professional work, and generates funds for schools.

the economy: control centers

It increases new types of education programs, as employers and other groups take over the job that public schools normally perform inadequately—that of educating a skilled work force.

International competition in growth has driven some nations to a drastic overhaul of their educational systems. Britain, after the demise of the Empire and the Commonwealth, found it necessary to convert its more aristocratic and obsolete educational system into one that would produce, in the new Red Brick colleges and non-elite schools, technically trained manpower to accelerate economic growth. Communist nations have transformed their educational systems in a similar manner and, especially in the post-Sputnik era, American education has overhauled and placed new stress on scientific and technological training as a means to strengthen its military-economic potential.

Investment

Much sense and nonsense has been written about investment in education. It is suggested that economic productivity is more a result of investment in education and human resources than in hardware and technology. Some experts say that the economy needs the boost of a new growth industry—education, and that large sums should be invested in schools to provide jobs and stimulate economic activities.

The investment theory is relatively new. Americans generally believe in the value of education to the *individual*, and employers have seen the value to them of investment in job training, but only recently have economists begun to calculate the value of general education to the economy. The basic idea can be traced to more remote sources. Adam Smith, for example, postulated that the division of labor was the source of wealth of nations, and that the skills needed to perform specialized labor are the result of "habit, custom and education." [2]

Schools and the economy interact, each influencing the other. Viewed as an investment, education is an independent variable, influencing rather than being influenced by what transpires in the economic system. Treating education as an independent variable, Charles Benson comments, "the strength of nations is measured to a significant degree by their rates of economic growth" and policymakers are now more likely to "consider education (or 'training,' as it is sometimes called) a strategic variable in planning for economic improvement." [3]

Theodore Schultz claims that education is a form of capital and that as such, "it has grown in Western societies at a much faster rate than conventional (non-human) capital, and that its growth may well be the most distinctive feature of the economic system." [4]

Contributions of education are variously computed. It is estimated that from 1899 to 1952, four-fifths of our economic growth came from improvements in national efficiency—technology, organization, and human capital—and only about one-fifth from conventional inputs of land, labor, and capital. During the period 1929–1957, according to Edward Denison, education accounted for 23 percent of growth in national income and for 42 percent of growth in national income per person employed.[5] "The contribution of education to eco-

[2] Adam Smith, *Wealth of Nations* (New York: Modern Library, 1937), p. 15.
[3] Charles S. Benson, *Perspectives on the Economics of Education* (Boston: Houghton Mifflin, 1963), p. 3.
[4] Theodore Schultz, "Investment in Human Capital," in Benson, *op. cit.,* p. 12.
[5] Edward F. Denison, in Seymour Harris, *Education and Public Policy* (Berkeley, California: McCutchan, 1965), pp. 328–347.

39

nomic growth" in those years, according to Theodore Schultz, "exceeded that of physical capital." [6]

Despite these calculations, those who invest in machinery and physical capital often oppose public investment in education. Direct profit to business from good schools is apparent in the inclination of employers to move to areas where the supply of trained personnel is abundant. It can also be seen in the effort of states to attract business by investing in schools and higher education. The early boom in high quality industry in California, for example, can be attributed partially to a statewide system of free public colleges and to high teacher salaries. Similarly, in the East, development is based on a symbiotic relation between Ivy League universities and the industries of the Eastern urban strip.

For some economically depressed areas, much hope is placed in education. Radical improvements in Southern schools are believed necessary to make the South competitive with other areas.

Non-economic demands also stimulate educational investments—among them: popular faith in the value of education for self-improvement, general consumer demand for education as pleasure and recreation in a society of increasing leisure, demands of disadvantaged for equality through education, desire of many educators for increased investments for both personal and altruistic reasons.

An Agricultural Model

Investment in agricultural education and productivity in the United States pre-dated and fed the industrial revolution. The "total system" of education and research-development contributing to the phenomenal increase in agricultural production was

> . . . a universal system of elementary education producing literacy for almost everyone and also some acquaintance with agricultural procedures. A system of agricultural high schools extending into practically every important agricultural community in the country, training hundreds of thousands of boys and girls to be experts in all phases of agricultural life. A system of agricultural colleges covering the entire country and providing for agricultural leadership and producing highly trained personnel. A system of agricultural experimental and research stations covering every section of the country, and dealing at a very high, advanced technical level with all kinds of problems facing the farmer. Finally, a system of adult and extension education reaching back into the local communities, taking the technical information back to the farmer and his wife . . . it has been amazingly successful.[7]

Federally subsidized land grant colleges were so absorbed with rural education that the training of "mechanics" with which they were also charged, was neglected. Funds invested by other sources more directly spurred industrial growth. About a century ago the first engineering school was opened and since then several hundred more. Industry itself has supported thousands of research and development laboratories, which have employed some 200,000 technical people and hundreds of thousands of assistants. "Everything indicates that the larger these expenditures become, the more profitable they are, and the more the reason to expand them even further. . . . In some of the newer fields, e.g.,

---

[6] Theodore Schultz, "Reflections on Investment in Man," *Journal of Political Economics*, Part II, Special Supplement (October, 1962), 3.
[7] Harold F. Clark, "The Return on Educational Investment," in Benson, *op. cit.*, p. 28.

electronics and aviation, industries are dependent almost entirely upon their developmental and research programmes." [8]

Differential Productivity

Though education's contribution to the economy has risen sharply since the turn of the century, it does not rise at a constant rate and is expected by some to decline the last decades of the century unless the quality of education improves. The society no doubt will find alternate ways to provide quality job and professional training if the schools cannot meet the need.[9]

Opinions differ on the type and amount of investment to be made and the productivity of additional increments of investment. How productive, for example, would one year of free college for the entire United States population be compared with one year of free pre-school? Would investment be more productive in science and technology than in other fields? For some groups more than other groups? For the poor more than the rich?

Benson says:

Where the schooling made available to some groups falls below conventional standards, there are likely to be economic gains in closing the gap. For example, increased expenditures for resources on elementary education in some parts of the South would probably offer very high returns. Next, duration is basic to the advance of knowledge, and scientific knowledge is itself the basis of improvements in techniques of production in many industries today. Lastly, a sharp rise in the quality of education offered by the schools over the whole country should produce economic returns, but it is not possible to specify what skills and attributes would be created or precisely how they would be used.[10]

Simply keeping youth in school for longer periods without giving them specific job skills or adding significant knowledge might in fact reduce total productivity by delaying their entry into the job market. Intangibles and non-job related consequences of investment are difficult to assess, as for example the effect on youth aspirations at all grade levels of opening college opportunities, and the impact of school investment on society's general intellectual sophistication. Educational investment contributes more to long-term than short-term growth because of the time lag between investment and return. The measurement of productivity is therefore delayed and difficult.

Investment in mass education is desirable for various reasons. Providing unlimited education to everyone at public expense, "may seem generous but the American propensity in this direction may not be so wild economically as the critics would have us believe." It may be that "raising the general level of 'intelligence' is quite as important economically as developing a few top performers." [11]

Over-Investment

Though some nations have, for current use, an educated "surplus" and others a "shortage," literacy and industrialization are very highly correlated when industrialization is measured by the proportion of jobs.[12]

[8] Clark, *ibid.*, p. 29.
[9] Edward F. Denison, *op. cit.*, pp. 328–347.
[10] Benson, *op. cit.*, p. 4.
[11] Harold M. Groves, "Education and Economic Growth," in Benson, *op. cit.*, p. 12.
[12] Hilda Hertz Golden, "Literacy and Social Change in Underdeveloped Countries," *Rural Sociology* (February, 1955), 1:20, 1–7.

41

Japan, the most industrialized and rapidly growing nation in the East, has a system of universal public education which has produced the most literate population in Asia.

The mass societies—the United States, U.S.S.R., and China—have made heavy investments in mass and higher education. The communist nations have considered such investment a prerequisite to the industrial "leap forward." For them, investment in education has had higher economic priority than investment in consumer goods. They have also allocated a much larger share of resources to polytechnical education. In a society where the governing bureaucracy of both the political and economic systems is dominated by engineers—in contrast to the United States and Britain where lawyers tend to dominate—emphasis on technological education flows from values of the elite.

The two Germanies typify the difference between systems. West Germans claim that East Germans over-invest in education, needlessly reducing the work force, making education another casual consumer good, and wasting resources on trained personnel who then want to migrate out of the country.[13] Differences may not be so great as assumed however, considering the vast network of educational institutions maintained by West Germany outside the schools, including worker and adult education, and vocational training. The assertion, then, that West Germany has the highest productivity in Europe and, relatively the lowest educational opportunities, seems misleading.[14]

Developing Areas

An index based on enrollments in secondary and higher education was devised by two economists.[15] Applied to 75 developing nations, the index correlated highly with Gross National Product, the percentage of agricultural workers, and other indices of growth and modernization. The 75 areas all had critical shortages in all categories of high-level manpower. Among African nations, which were at the lowest level, about 20 percent of the students had finished primary school, less than one percent of the population had finished senior secondary school, and over half of the existing high-level manpower were "expatriates" (foreigners).

Though the survey favored raising the quality of primary education rather than expanding it, other economists and many of the local people favor *more* rather than *better* primary education. More adult education is recommended by the survey as a necessary stimulant to the initial stages of agricultural development which will, in turn, trigger industrial development.

Western planners suggest an economic strategy of concentration on agricultural rather than industrial development in the next decades, though many developing nations want to "leap forward" directly into industrialization. Schultz claims that in developing areas investment in human resources is likely to be underrated or neglected, partly as a result of our own growth doctrines which

[13] Other developed nations have lost their educated through migration, where it is permitted—notably Britain which has suffered a serious "brain drain" to the United States, Australia and Canada. Some nations such as Egypt have expanded education but closed the doors to emigration.

[14] Extension of formal education in West Germany has been restricted by the resistance of elite teachers of the Gymnasium who oppose opening secondary schools to the less "gifted" and whose voice is strong in German education; it has also been limited by the fact that religious political parties and regions of large Roman Catholic populations have not given much support to public education.

[15] Frederick Harbison and Charles A. Myers, *Education, Manpower and Economic Growth: Strategies of Human Resource Development* (New York: McGraw-Hill, 1964).

the economy: control centers

"assign the stellar role to the formation of nonhuman capital, and take as an obvious fact the superabundance of human resources." [16] It is not possible, he says, for these nations to have the fruits of a modern agriculture and the abundance of modern industries without making large investments in human beings.

Some developing nations, on the other hand, "tend to become excessively interested in pouring their limited resources into education," says Seymour Harris.[17] Some countries, such as Ghana, have over-invested in expensive higher education for prestige purposes. Others have permitted excessive investment in less useful professional training—particularly law, classical liberal arts, and prestige studies that are remnants of colonial rule.

Other Considerations

Basic components of prosperity, according to R. D. Baldwin, are: "(1) Perhaps most important—free, stable, democratic government. No modern economy can flourish on the shifting sands of political institutions which bind the many to the wishes of the few. (2) Abundant natural resources in both materials and men. Prosperity is unthinkable unless material and human resources are available. (3) Some systematic, dependable means of fusing material and human resources, under stabilized democratic auspices, into the dynamics of high-energy civilization." [18] The education system, he says, is or should be central to development in that it trains the work force and prepares citizens for stable, democratic government.

The relative contribution of various educational media to economic development cannot be calculated. Perhaps the *schools* (beyond basic education) account for only a small part of the total, while other media—job training, military training, the mass media, experience, and so forth—account for the larger part. Even if the school's contribution is large, its productivity may still be low and its contribution only a portion of the potential.

Manpower

Isolation and Integration

Early education was related to manpower needs only in that it prepared young aristocrats and clerics to assume their adult careers. A young aristocrat was to become a member of a small power elite and a leisure class; that is, he would not work much and never with his hands. He would be judged by his mastery of classical learning and his acquisition of the manners of a gentleman. In 1642, for example, the entrance requirements for Harvard were: "When any schollar is able to understand *Tully,* or such like classical Latine Author *extempore,* and make and speake true Latine in Verse and Prose, *suo et aiunt* Marte; And decline perfectly the Paradigm's of *Nounes* and *Verbes* in the *Greek* tongue: Let him then and not before be capable of admission into the Colledge." [19]

Industrialization introduced a multitude of new manpower training needs. In the United States, however, vocational and technological education have

[16] Schultz, *op. cit.,* p. 19.
[17] Seymour E. Harris, *Challenge and Change in American Education* (Berkeley, Calif.: McCutchan, 1965), p. 8.
[18] Baldwin, *op. cit.,* p. 20.
[19] *New England's First Fruits* (London, 1643), Mass. Hist. Col., 1792, Vol. I, pp. 242–246, as quoted in Cubberley, *Readings in the History of Education,* p. 292.

been outside the domain of most public schools and even, to an extent, institutions of higher learning. Nowhere in the world is so much liberal arts training given to so many for so long (and with so little effect, some would say) as in American schools up to the graduate level. In the U.S.S.R., by contrast, work-related subjects are part of the curriculum from early grades, and work-study programs have been so heavily stressed that for a period all college students were required to participate. The functions of this stress on work have been to teach the habit of hard labor, fill manpower needs, prepare students for specific vocations, and prevent the rise of a new leisure—and perhaps dissident—class of students. In industrializing, most nations have put heavy stress on teaching work habits and the value of hard and regular labor.

Reassessment of manpower training needs resulted from both Sputnik and civil rights agitation. Together they stimulated the first large-scale federal peacetime effort at manpower training and recruitment. Most of the training programs generated were outside the schools, though considerable spill-over occurred into school industrial arts and vocational programs.

Manpower and Training

While a primary function of the education system is to provide qualified manpower to the economic system, problems arise in performing this task adequately, among them: (1) Manpower training needs are not properly planned and programmed; (2) schools exist in such isolation that known manpower training needs may not be transmitted to them; (3) even when transmitted, the schools usually cannot respond with suitable training programs. Since vocational education in the schools has been notoriously obsolete, it is questionable whether schools are suitable institutions for preparing manpower for specific vocations. Such training has been of highest quality when school study programs have been integrated with on-the-job training. Internship programs of medical schools offer models in higher education for effective on-the-job training. Schools of education and some other professional schools have been justifiably criticized for failure to establish internship programs that match medical training in depth and scope.

Business and industry offer about as much vocational training, from the simplest to the most advanced, as all institutions of higher learning combined. Some industries also subsidize the tuition of employees studying outside the plant. Such practices are most conspicuous in industries such as aviation, automation, and electronics, which receive heavy federal subsidies and consume much skilled labor.[20] Federal funds have subsidized many innovative efforts in manpower training, at the highest and lowest levels.[21]

Education and Training

Training may be regarded as distinct from education in that it prepares for specific job skills. The separation of the two has had serious consequences for both. Much of the obsolescence and impracticality of education can be attributed to its separation from training and jobs, and much of the narrowness of training programs results from their failure to use training as a base for reaching higher learning. Job performance can, for example, be

[20] In 1964 North American Aviation, as part of a union negotiated contract, paid 102,-000 employees for 1,154,000 hours of study completed.
[21] The Manpower Development & Training Act (MDTA), between its passage in 1962 and 1966, trained about 625,000 unemployed workers. The National Development Education Act (NDEA), passed in 1958 after Sputnik, was aimed at producing highly trained manpower. In 1963 it represented about one-fourth of all federal expenditures on education.

44

used for literacy and mathematical education, and for teaching various operations of the industrial and economic system. Work-study programs have tried to join the two, but often they do not use the specific job requirements to build general education. In the typical school, instructors in "academic" departments seldom know or care about what their students are studying in vocational courses, and vocational teachers are similarly isolated.

Employment Trends

Employment is shifting rapidly toward more skilled and fewer manual jobs. Professional and technical workers were 6.6 percent of the employed in 1947 and 12.2 percent in 1964. Although only 15 percent of Americans wore white collars in 1900, by 1940 the figure was 28.5 percent and by 1970 it is expected to be 48 percent. Of these, about seven out of ten will be managerial, professional, or technical, the new backbone of the upper and middle class.

The main reason for the increase of white-collar jobs is the rapid growth of those industries—education, finance, insurance, health, and business services —which employ predominantly white-collar and professional workers. The most fertile area for public policy initiative appears to be in the professions. In education, for example, the number of teachers is expanding four times faster than the general population, and new types of job categories are required to permit less highly trained personnel to take over some tasks traditionally performed by teachers.

Jobs requiring no secondary education decreased 25 percent in the past decade. During the next decade the fastest growth will be in occupations requiring the most training and education. About one half of all jobs now open to high school graduates were not there when the graduates were in the sixth grade and will not be there in ten years.

A record 26 million new young workers will enter the job market during the 'sixties. This phenomenal increase will accompany an actual decrease in the age group 35–44.

Table 2

Estimated Male Population Changes, 1960–1970

Age	Percentage
14–24	46.4
25–34	11.5
35–44	−3.2
45–54	10.8
55–64	19.1
65 and over	5.5

Such population shifts can be expected to significantly affect both school and society and increase the power of the youth group. Estimates differ on the relative impact of manpower training programs, public policy initiatives, and economic growth on employment rates. A major report on economic progress suggested that public policy alone can more than offset technological change. Its public policy recommendations included: government acting as an "employer of last resort, directing its efforts to fill community and social needs; a floor under family income for the poor; compensatory education for the disadvantaged; creation of a national computerized job-matching system to provide information on local, regional and national levels; application of new technology

45

to Medicare, education, air and water pollution, transport, housing, increased use of systems analysis in resolving social and environmental problems." [22]

Recommendations for school policy were: defer vocational training until after high school, offer free two-year college to all—both technical and community. "The two types of schools might in many instances be merged into a community education center offering both the theoretical foundations of trade, technical, and business occupations and the opportunity to 'earn-by-doing' while pursuing liberal education or semi-professional training." [23] It favored a "system of education that is open-ended, with freedom for mature students to enter, leave when alternative experiences seem more fruitful, and then reenter." [24]

Since manpower needs are great and since the education and training of highly qualified personnel cannot be done on a short-term basis, Gottfried Bombach suggests forecasting and disseminating information by an impartial authority responsible for the entire country, which would supply the individual with the needed employment-market guidance for the distant future.[25]

Long-term comprehensive national budgets, including projections of national goals, education needs, development of physical and human resources, and public spending, are also proposed as a means of forecasting and planning to replace the present annual and more fragmented Presidential budgets.

Financing Education

Needs

If the schools are to pursue their traditional role, expanding rather than changing in any basic way, funds must be found to at least equal that expansion. The dimensions of current needs are vast. In 1962, one of four public school classrooms was obsolete, and one of three children had no kindergarten, let alone nursery school, to attend. Some 248,000 new teachers were needed in 1965, or 118,000 more than the number of college graduates who would accept teaching jobs.

Teaching staff in public schools rose 56 percent in the decade beginning in 1955, and the college age population, which will increase 50 percent during the 'seventies (up to 7 million youths), will make new demands on higher education. The proportion of secondary students is rising and the per unit costs for high school students is about 60 percent more than for elementary students.

Expenditures

Some $14 billion was spent in the year 1953–54 on education at all levels, public and private.[26] This figure rose 150 percent to $35 billion in 1963–64. The largest increase was in funds going to public colleges.

In 1963–64, $10 billion was spent on higher education, triple the amount

[22] National Commission on Technology, Automation and Economic Progress, *Technology and the American Economy*, I (February, 1966), 46.

[23] *Ibid.*, p. 46.

[24] *Ibid.*, p. 47. The estimate of potential sources of new jobs in public service was 5.3 million, including 1.2 million in medical institutions and health services, 1.1 million in educational institutions, and 1.3 million in national beautification.

[25] Gottfried Bombach, "Manpower Forecasting and Educational Policy," *Sociology of Education* (Fall, 1965), 38:5, 343–374.

[26] This compares with $7 billion spent on advertising in 1951. In 1958, 13.1 billion was spent on public elementary and secondary schools, 15.6 billion on alcoholic beverages and tobacco, 30.4 billion on auto purchase and operation, and 17.0 billion on various types of recreation.

spent a decade earlier. In 1953–54, $9 billion was spent on public elementary and secondary education and ten years later the figure had risen to $21 billion.[27]

In 1929–30 only 2½ percent of the GNP was spent on education. By 1949–50 this had risen to 5 percent, but ten years later it was down to 4 percent.[28] While total tax revenues have risen 935 percent since 1930, revenues for education increased only 435 percent.

In 1929 the states bore about 17 percent of school costs, by 1947 about 30 percent, and by 1965 about 50 percent.

Revenues to schools from federal sources were about 4 percent of the total in 1965, a rise of only about 1 percent over the preceding decade. By 1970, the figure is expected to rise to about 15 percent. Over 40 federal agencies, however, spend money on education, though not on the public schools. The military carries on the largest of the federal educational efforts, and anti-poverty programs are directed mainly at education. About 20 percent of the income of higher education is derived from federal government sources, and federal funds support about 70 percent of research at universities. Of the total federal budget in 1965, 51 billion went to national defense, 28 billion to health, education, and welfare, and 1.5 billion to education.

Productivity

How successful are the schools in producing desired educational results? Could other methods of organization do better for less? One view is that only money can improve the schools, the other extreme is that money will yield only more of the same results. Relative to other child care costs, such as baby sitters, the schools are economical and efficient. Baby sitter fees of $1.50 per hour for the care of one child during school hours would be $1,350.00 or about three times as much as is spent per pupil by the schools. Higher education spends two and three times per pupil the amount spent by the public schools. On the other hand it can be said that at $500 per pupil for a class of 35, the school spends the tidy sum of $17,500 per class per annum.

Ideally, funds invested in education would produce the efficiency of operation which industrial investments have often produced, that is, unit costs would be reduced through technological and organizational change at the same time that quantity of production would be increased and, presumably, quality raised. Efficiency will be further discussed in Chapter Six.

[27] National Education Association, *Financial Status of the Public Schools* (Washington, D. C., 1964).

[28] John Vaizey, *The Economics of Education* (London: Faber and Faber, 1962).

stratification:
classrooms
in a class society
five

Stratification is a hierarchical or rank ordering of social assets. It is found in all societies and almost all the sub-systems and organizations included in them, but in varying degree and kind. In colonial America the General Court of Massachusetts in 1651 declared its "utter detestation and dislike that men and women of meane Conditions should take upon themselves the garb of gentlemen, by wearing gold or silver lace or buttons, or points at their knees or to walk in bootes . . . which though allowable to persons of greater estates, or more liberal education, yet we cannot but judge it intollerable in persons of such like conditions." [1] The American Revolution declared that "all men are created equal" and tried to free the new society that it created from its colonial heritage, so that all men could wear "silver lace" if they chose but trusting they would not choose to acquire the airs of aristocrats.

Stratification appears in its most "ideal" form in the military where rank, authority, and privilege are clearly noted by title, uniform, pay, duties, and where *class* divisions are so explicitly drawn that "officers" can neither live, eat, nor carry on social relations with "the men." It is essentially a three-class society. In the Army, sergeants and middle-men stand between officers and enlisted men, much as the foreman stands between "boss" and "worker" in the shop,

[1] Jernegan, *American Colonies, 1492–1750* (New York: Longmans, Green, 1929), pp. 179–180.

priest between hierarchy and parishioners in the church, and teacher between decision-makers and students in the schools. In these cases, the "middle" class often acts as an agent for, or an ally with, its "superiors."

Some people believe that social stratification, as we know it, is ordained by forces beyond our control—by God, by the nature and innate inequality of man, or by the necessities of organization. Such speculation does not take into account the flexibility of human institutions or the historical upward thrust of the dispossessed. The other side claims, with Carl Sandburg, that "money is like manure—good only when spread around," and that the most efficient and desirable industrial society is the one with the least stratification.

The traditional stratification system of Western man, based on ancestral status, was shaken by the industrial revolution. The city, the assembly line, and opportunities in the new world offered many people a chance to acquire property and status. It did not give everyone the *same* opportunity. Of two men with equal ambition and ability, the man whose father was a banker usually progressed much farther than one whose father cleaned the bank offices. But room at the top opened, and upward mobility for many people became possible.

The shift from ascribed to achieved status benefited not only the ambitious individual but also a society that needed men of ability as well as pedigree. It left the impression with many, however, that "ability" was all that counted, and that everyone began at the same starting line and had an equal chance to achieve. If some failed to reach the mark of others, it was assumed to be their own fault, and in no sense a result of inequities in the system. It is this assumption, as applied to the schools, that must be examined.

Class

The voluminous literature on stratification contains a good deal of haggling over the number of "classes" (or groupings of strata) and their composition. The inspiration for much of this is the Marxian assertion that *relationship to the means of production* is the most significant class division, whether or not people are conscious of class membership. Essentially two classes are formed by this relationship: those who work for others (the proletariat) and those who own and operate (the bourgeoisie). These are economic and power classes. Refutations of the Marxian schema have usually dealt with "class" divisions based on conscious identity of interest and similarities in occupation, status, or style of life. Researchers have usually found five or six of these "classes" in any given community.

Both classifications are useful. In contrast to the animal realm, man is infinitely complex and needs many classifications to distinguish among the various social groups to which he belongs. Moreover, these classes must take account of the variability of human behavior in place and time. In education, economic groups are often relevant to discussions of power in the schools, and status groups more to discussions of cultural differences among students and families; both are relevant to stratification and both can be seen to affect who gets what in the schools.

School stratification has occupied more of the attention of sociologists than any other educational topic, probably because of the strategic role of schools in stratifying people and choosing elites, the primary value attached to equal educational opportunity contrasted with the obvious *in*equalities in the school, and the social unrest generated by these inequities.

Many, perhaps most, major changes in the schools have been produced by pressures from the disadvantaged for more and better education—changes

49

that include school expansion, curriculum changes to provide a more practical education to the disadvantaged, addition of new school functions in health, recreation, counseling, and so forth. These pressures have made social and racial stratification the most prominent issue in modern education.

Sociological inquiries into community and school have found various stratification systems. Robert and Helen Lynd found in Middletown a two-class system, composed essentially of businessmen and workers.[2] August Hollingshead found a six-class stratification sytem in Elmtown's high school, one that gave rewards to students based on their family's class position.[3] Those from "upper class' families received the greatest rewards (honors, good marks, extracurricular benefits, elected office, etc.), and those from the lower strata received most of the punishment (reprimands, expulsion, demerits, poor marks, etc.).

Virtually all studies have found that the success of students in school is directly related to their class background. Such unequal achievement may be attributable to one or all of the variables which we will examine: systematic stratification and inequality in school and society, the natural ability of students, the culture and motivation of students and their families.

Higher Education

The Degree Elite

Higher education occupies the peak of the educational —and, increasingly, the social—hierarchy of institutions. It controls much that goes on below it, in elementary and secondary schools, and much that goes on beyond it, in the society. It is said indeed to be the control center of the New Society, an emerging version of Plato's *Republic*, run by scholars and a "degree elite" of professionals, technicians, and other holders of college diplomas. About 76 percent of top executives of the 600 largest non-financial corporations had college degrees in 1964 (91 percent had *some* college), compared to 62 percent in 1950. The biggest change was in the number with graduate work, up from 17 percent to 31 percent, and the number with technical degrees was up from 20 percent to 33 percent.[4] One study found, however, that there was an inverse relation between educational attainment and executives and the rate of growth of their firms.[5]

Higher education determines the society's stratification system and influences most institutions through the training of the personnel who direct them. It even trains the personnel managers who hire people based on "qualifications" conferred by higher education. Such training makes it unlikely that those who hire will use other criteria for selecting the "qualified."

The role of higher education is to select the "able" from the lower schools, give them a certificate (and presumably an education) which will serve as a kind of achieved "pedigree," opening a place for them in the elite of managers, professionals, and owners who, in turn, stand at the peak of society's hierarchy.

2 Robert S. Lynd and Helen Merrell Lynd, *Middletown, A Study in American Culture* (New York: Harcourt, Brace, 1929).

3 August Hollingshead, *Elmtown's Youth* (New York: John Wiley, 1949).

4 "The Big Business Executive—1964," published by *Scientific American* (1965), a study of presidents, chairmen or executive vice presidents of 600 of the largest non-financial corporations.

5 W. Lloyd Warner and James C. Abeglen, *Occupational Mobility in American Business and Industry, 1928–1952* (Minnesota: University of Minnesota Press, 1955).

stratification: classrooms in a class society

Despite the general assumption that such pedigrees are based exclusively on demonstrated ability, compared to older ones of birth and ancestry, it appears that among educational institutions the greatest inequality and unachieved status exist in higher education. These institutions tend, even more than others, to exclude those from lower-income groups with demonstrated or latent ability. Of high school graduates in 1960 who decided not to go to college, 42 percent said finances played a part in that decision, and half of this group (over 200,000 students) said they could not afford even to consider college.

Among twelfth graders, 29 percent of the boys and 54 percent of the girls in the two aptitude deciles were not even enrolled in high school-college prep courses; 31 percent of the boys and 50 percent of the girls in this top group said they did not plan to go to college.[6] These students are overwhelmingly from lower income groups.

When the costs of college are not prohibitive for many able lower-income students, arbitrarily high "standards" set by many low-cost public colleges often are. Hence, these able students cannot even enter college. There is, in fact, an absence of evidence that the most able in performance of jobs or other real-life tasks are selected or produced by the standards set and training offered by higher education. Employers often hire from among the degree elite because of the prestige rather than the superior training or job performance skill attached to a college degree.

Public schools attended by lower-income students usually do not prepare them for college entrance, often because both the school and the students see that college doors are closed. Such schools not only commonly fail to inspire students with desire to overcome financial obstacles and "make it" to college, but often discourage such aspirations as unrealistic when they are self-generated. Often the costs of college are so high and standards so arbitrarily set that they are indeed unrealistic. Many high schools in low-income areas do not offer the courses needed to qualify students for admission to their own state universities.

In only a few cases have colleges tried to compensate for the inferior preparation of these students, aid preparatory institutions, make allowances for such handicaps in admissions, or create programs to "hold" lower-income students after admission. Indeed many colleges give admission preferences and automatic approval to students from upper-income schools, and few make it financially feasible for the less-advantaged to attend college with as much ease as the advantaged.

It apparently cannot be said with any statistical authority what proportion of lower-strata youth actually enter college and stay there. Even the large federally financed Project Talent surveyed college aspirants in the twelfth grade, a level that the great majority of lower-income youth never reach.[7]

A national survey of Negroes, one of the lowest income groups, reported that over half of all Negro college students attend largely segregated institutions in the South and Southwest, and that about 4.6 percent of college students are Negro, compared to the 9 percent representation of Negroes in the general population.[8] About 75 percent of all institutions of higher learning have less than 2 percent Negro student enrollment. Negroes attend colleges that have fewer PhD's on the faculty and where faculty salaries are lower than at other colleges. They are more likely to enter the state college than the more prestigious state university system, attend schools with low tuition and high dropout rates,

[6] Project Talent, survey by the University of Pittsburgh.
[7] Project Talent, op. cit.
[8] U.S. Department of Health, Education, and Welfare, Office of Education, *Equality of Educational Opportunity* (Washington, D. C.: Government Printing Office).

and major in relatively few subjects (engineering, agriculture, education, social work, social science, nursing).

Regional opportunities vary. It appears that the far West offers the best chance for college. California has operated a vast multiversity and system of community colleges which are both close to home and inexpensive. In 1961 California spent $42.70 per capita on higher education, Michigan $30.60, Georgia $13.30, New York $10.80, New Jersey $8.70, Pennsylvania $7.60, and Massachusetts $5.90. Over a third of all colleges in the Pacific states admit all high school graduates, but only 6 percent in the Middle Atlantic states. In about a fourth of all colleges (35 percent in 1960 and 25 percent in 1965) only a high school diploma is needed for entrance, providing an open system for lower-income students which is marred by the practice of setting quotas, usually small ones, on the number who will pass into the sophomore year.

Some of the basic statistics on college opportunity are either missing or misleading. Even the proportion of youth age 18 to 24 (dropouts as well as high school graduates) who attend college is often reported as 35 or 40 percent. In fact, only 22 percent of 18 to 24-year-olds were in college in 1960, a figure that represents a world's record but which is considerably less than what is often reported or what the nation can afford. The figure is expected to rise to 29 percent by 1970 and 40 percent by 1985.

EQUALIZATION. Low college tuition offers few opportunities to lower-income students if entrance "standards" are too high to hurdle. Tuition-free but with "high standards," the city colleges in New York City have, for example, subsidized many middle-income students and virtually excluded most impoverished ethnic groups. At the University of Michigan, a low tuition but "high standards" state school, only 25 percent of the fathers of freshmen had less than a college education and only 4.8 percent had less than a high school diploma. Average family income was in excess of $15,000, and only 1.8 percent of students came from families below $4,000 per year, the poverty line.[9]

Thus, vast public subsidies underwrite the education of middle- and upper-income students. About a quarter to a third of all non-tuition money spent on education in the United States is spent on higher education, mainly for the advantaged. Even scholarships and student loans favor those who are rather well-off. Of 8,000 scholarship winners in 65 leading institutions, only 1,200 went to students from families with incomes below $5,000.[10]

In the U.S.S.R. tuition is virtually free and students admitted to college are given living stipends, but when entrance "standards" are high, as they are in the U.S.S.R., this too can be a regressive system, subsidizing the well-off and excluding the low-income. Similar arrangements result in serious class inequities in many nations. In the German Federal Republic, for example, workers were 56.6 percent of the population and 6 percent of the total college population.[11]

The American college nevertheless has expanded to offer some opportunities to the common man. Once a completely exclusive reserve, colleges found a new role when the Civil War produced the "cow colleges," the agricultural schools, of the Morrill Act. From this seed came the massive growth of higher education, a new and more "plebeian" student body, and a greater preference

9 "The Student Body at the University of Michigan, 1963," a UMSEU research document, mimeographed.
10 American Council on Education Survey Report.
11 "Arbeitgemainschaft Deutscher Lehrerverbande," WCOTP Theme Study (Addis Ababa, Ethiopia, 1965), p. 43.

stratification: classrooms in a class society

for the practical over the theological, aristocratic, and classical. Aware that the commonweal and national survival depended on higher education, federal intervention since then has often been in the name of national security. Some federal programs have offered opportunities to the disadvantaged, but most have not. The GI Bill, the most egalitarian of federal programs gave college subsidies to all veterans and markedly changed student bodies. But usually, aid to higher education has gone to middle- and upper-income groups. Even the NDEA effort to prepare students in high school for "advanced placement" in college aided upper-income groups.[12]

ANTI-INTELLECTUALISM. A commencement speaker at an early Harvard graduation said that without the college's presence, "The ruling class would have been subjected to mechanics, cobblers, and tailors; the gentry would have been overwhelmed by lewd fellows of the baser sort, the sewage of Rome, the dregs of an illiterate plebs which judgeth much from emotion, little from truth." Anti-intellectualism, assumed to be endemic in American life, may be as much a product of stratified higher education as of the excessive envy and ignorance of "lewd fellows" and "cobblers."

One British view suggests the resentment to the degree elite that may exist: "The voice of privilege and command of those days [the war years] spoke often in a tone controlled more by sniffishness than by manly love of the flag. You will not eat our food, wear our clothes, enter our clubs; you will not speak until spoken to for you are not *a college man.* Had the Harvard lieutenants and Bowdoin ensigns tipped a universal wink millions would have had a less exacerbating encounter with 'trained minds.' Conceivably the resentment and frustration thus amassed—anger at university smugness known at first hand— wasn't an insignificant part of the huge capital drawn on by mind-baiters in the Hiss and McCarthy years." [13] Largely due to the appeal of some educated statesmen and the obviously growing reliance of the social system on men of knowledge, anti-intellectualism appears to be a receding feature of American life.

PRESTIGE COLLEGES. Colleges are also stratified. While a college diploma may admit one to the degree elite, a diploma from the "right" institution may admit the bearer to the pedigree elite. At the top of this stratified pyramid have been Ivy League, leading technical schools, and a few public universities. At the bottom have been segregated Southern Negro schools and community colleges. The "right" college offers "contact," assumed "competence," and the personal "quality" (style, manner, dress, behavior) of the elite.

In response to the intense striving of many students and parents for entry to the "right" institutions, various rankings of schools and departments have been made. Usually the highest on the lists have been those with the largest endowments, highest faculty salaries, or most attractive setting.

Albert H. Bowker rated graduate schools on scholastic merit. Among the top ten on two lists (one for science and the other social sciences-humanities) were Harvard, Columbia, Yale, Chicago, Stanford, Princeton, and California (Berkeley, the only public institution). A high correlation was found between ratings and faculty pay.[14] The American Council on Education asked 4,008 scholars to rank 106 schools giving doctoral degrees. Only 13 of these graduate

[12] R. F. Campbell and R. A. Bunnell, "Differential Impact of National Programs on Secondary Schools," *The School Review* (Winter, 1963), 474–476.
[13] George Lichtheim, "Introspectives," *New Statesman* (February 7, 1964).
[14] Albert H. Bowker, "Quality and Quantity in Higher Education," *Journal of American Statistical Association* (March, 1965).

stratification: classrooms in a class society

schools were rated as having "distinguished" faculties in more than one field of study. The 13 (in alphabetical order) were: California (Berkeley), Cal. Tech, Chicago, Columbia, Harvard, Illinois, MIT, Michigan, Princeton, Rockefeller, Stanford, Wisconsin, Yale. Ratings were done in five areas: humanities, social sciences, biological sciences, physical sciences, engineering.

Such rankings may be as much a figment of vanished or undeserved reputation as of real quality. As in public schools, it would seem advisable to gauge quality in these rankings by impact on students rather than simply arbitrary measures of faculty, facilities, and so forth. Many corporate executives, labor and political leaders, scientists, and United States Presidents have come from the lowest-ranking schools, and many of the most productive citizens, before the ascendancy of the degree elite and even since, have not been to college at all.

Though higher education is the guardian of the school's and the society's stratification system, no satisfactory system of public evaluation and accountability has been devised. Indeed, only the spottiest data about higher education are publicly available. A public accounting would include a review of stratification processes, including a survey of class origins of entering and graduating students and records of the performance and contributions made in *real life* by students trained in various colleges. It would also seem desirable to evaluate the effect on the performance of the disadvantaged in elementary and secondary schools when opportunities in higher education are clearly opened to them.

Stratification
in Elementary and Secondary Schools

Inequality

In general the more money a student's parents make, the more money will be spent on his education, despite some effort at public "compensatory" expenditures for the disadvantaged. Inequalities are found not only in higher education but also in elementary and secondary schools, and they are found both between school districts and within them.

BIG CITY. My book *Education and Income* reported on inequalities in one large city school system.[15] I found that money spent on schools there, and the quality of education offered, varied in direct proportion to the income of families in the school neighborhood. Inequalities were found in: quality and adequacy of school buildings and facilities, school and class overcrowding, quality of teaching staff, methods of testing and estimating pupil performance, methods of selecting and segregating children, quality of the secondary curriculum, vocational and educational counseling of students, opportunities for completion of secondary school and admission to college, use of school buildings by communities, enrollments in pre-first grade programs, health, recreation, and food service facilities, total costs of educating students. All of these had their correlates in the poorer school performance of lower-income students.

As in the South, efforts have been made since the time of this study to correct some of the serious imbalances, particularly by constructing new buildings in ghetto and low-income areas, but their effect on student performance cannot yet be gauged. Stratified student performance clearly rests on much more than physical facilities, although the impact of obviously inferior and

15 Patricia Cayo Sexton, *Education and Income, Inequality of Opportunity in the Public Schools* (New York: Viking Press, 1961).

stratification: classrooms in a class society

inhospitable facilities on the morale of students and teachers cannot be over-looked.

More money was spent in Big City on schools in upper- than in lower-income areas. In addition, large sums, amounting to about $700 per student each year in Big City, are "saved" on low-income students who drop out or are pushed out of secondary schools. The money saved was expended on higher-income students who stayed in school.

In another city, appropriations for school operating expenses were almost 25 percent greater per pupil in white than in Negro schools, teacher salaries were 18 percent higher, non-teaching operating expenses—clerical and main-tenance, salaries, supplies, textbooks—were 50 percent higher.[16]

A study of 490 schools in 41 cities showed that both teachers and prin-cipals in low socioeconomic status schools were less experienced and less satisfied in their jobs than in high status areas. School principals in the highest status areas were considerably more satisfied with their teachers. In the highest status areas, 17 percent of principals wanted a principalship of "more prestige," com-pared to 43 percent in the lowest. Forty-two percent of teachers in the lowest and 18 percent in highest status schools wanted a transfer to a school "in a better neighborhood." Teachers in the lowest status schools were on the average younger, less experienced, newer to the school and getting less pay. "Teaching performance, whether in respect to competence in subject matter, innovation, interest in pupils, cooperation with school personnel, teaching methods, or the maintenance of discipline, was found to be somewhat poorer in schools of low-est than of highest socioeconomic status." [17]

James Conant found, between slums and suburbs, gross inequities in money expended among school districts. Spending in suburbs was often twice as great as spending in adjacent city slums.

Rural, Urban, and Regional

The greatest inequities are found in contrasts between rural and urban school *districts* and between poor and rich *states*. The highest state outlay for schools is about three times greater than the lowest. The average national expenditure per pupil during 1963–64 was $455. New York, a rich state, spent $705 per pupil that year; Mississippi, a very poor state, spent $241, and Puerto Rico $140. Yet Mississippi spent a higher *proportion* of its income on education than New York.[18] The rate of increase in spending has been higher in poor states. In the decade preceding 1965, spending in the South rose 90 percent. Yet *absolute* differences between rich and poor states are increasing. Poor states also are less likely to have parochial or private schools to relieve tax burdens.

Even greater inequities are found between districts, though little is known on the subject. In 1953 the United States Office of Education published *Expenditures for Education at the Midcentury*, but did not keep this vital information current thereafter. The volume reported that in 1949–50 spending varied from $45 per pupil in one Alabama local school district to about $445 in a New York district, or more than nine times the Alabama figure. Even

[16] *Handbook of Chicago School Segregation*, 1963, compiled and edited by the Educa-tion Committee, Coordinating Council of Community Organizations.

[17] Robert E. Herriott and Nancy Hoyt St. John, *Social Class and the Urban School* (New York: John Wiley, 1966), p. 207.

[18] Mississippi was 13th among states in "effort" (proportion of income) put into schools and has a non-public school enrollment of 3.1 percent. New York ranks 29th in effort and has a non-public school enrollment of 22.6 percent.

55

within rich states, great disparities exist. In New York spending ranged from $88 in the lowest, to $445 in the highest district, and in California in 1961–62 from $257 to $1,262. In many countries with a national system of education these local differences are less serious.

The Underclass

Because of the locally based school and the inequality of resources among local districts, an underclass of those who live in poverty and send their children to grossly inferior schools has remained despite general affluence, producing a higher illiteracy rate in the United States than in comparably advanced nations. In 1965 more than eight million adults in the United States had less than five years of school. In 1870, 20 percent of the total population were illiterate (11.5 percent of whites and 79.9 percent of nonwhites). By 1952, only 2.5 percent of the population could neither read nor write (1.8 percent of whites and 10.2 percent of nonwhites). Two-thirds of the heads of families in poverty have less than an eighth grade education.

Of nonwhites in the labor force over 18 years in 1965, 37.6 percent had only an elementary education, 37.5 percent had completed high school, and 7 percent had four or more years of college. Comparable figures for white workers were: 21.6 percent, 60 percent, and 12.2 percent.[19]

In the mid-sixties, more than two million children attended schools with a heating plant incapable of maintaining a "comfortable environment" in the winter. More than 60,000 had classes in buildings with no electricity; about 185,000 attended schools without running water; about 12 million did not have hot water in wash rooms; more than half a million used outdoor toilets, and more than ten million attended schools classed as "deteriorating," some of them dangerously so. About one out of three were taught in "unsatisfactory" school buildings.

Race

In the United States class and race are highly correlated. Negroes, for example, tend to occupy the lower levels of the stratification system in school and society. Their influence in the education system, such as it is, has come about through: the increase of their participation in the political and economic systems; geographic mobility from farm to city; the shift in race relations emphasis from education against prejudice to legislation against discrimination, and then to organization for social action, often centered on the school.

Civil rights programs during the 'sixties included demands for both *integrated* and *quality* education. Integrationists asserted that quality education for Negroes and whites could come only through integrated schools. The other side argued that, since school desegregation had been achieved for so few, emphasis should be on raising the quality of education in ghetto schools, hoping this would lead to eventual integration. In 1965 more than 65 percent of all Negro pupils in the first grade attended schools that were between 90 and 100 percent Negro; 87 percent in the first grade, and 66 percent in the twelfth grade attended schools that were 50 percent or more Negro.[20]

Breakthroughs in federal aid supported new compensatory education programs for the disadvantaged, and efforts were made to withhold federal funds from segregated schools, bus students into desegregated schools, redistrict to

[19] Christopher Jencks, "Education; the Racial Gap," *New Republic* (October 1, 1966), 24.

[20] *Equality of Educational Opportunity, op. cit.,* p. 3

stratification: classrooms in a class society

achieve better social balance, and create educational parks to bring various racial groups together. The de facto segregation of Northern schools as well as the de jure segregation of Southern schools came to public attention.

Parental demands centered on raising student achievement and reading scores, and to a lesser extent college entry. In verbal and non-verbal skills, Negroes were 1.6 years behind whites in the sixth grade; 2.4 years behind in the ninth grade, and 3.3 years behind in the twelfth.[21] Two-thirds of the 18-year old Negroes who took the armed forces tests in an 18-month period (in the mid-sixties) failed, compared to 18.8 percent of non-Negroes. High correlations were found between money spent on education and the performance of these 18-year olds. Mississippi and South Carolina rated 51st and 49th in salaries paid to teachers, and 49th and 50th in test performance. Negroes also turned their attention to gaining representation in power centers, participation in school decision-making, and employment within schools and related institutions as non-professionals.

The discontent of Negroes with public schools resulted in a reported 40 percent of all Negro white-collar workers sending their children to Catholic parochial or other private schools.[22] Attendance at parochial schools was most marked in Southern cities. Many of these schools became, by decision of high church authority, the most desegregated schools in the South.

Power
and the Stratification Process

In molding children to a stratified society, the school engages in continuous sorting and selecting of students—rating, ranking, and separating them into various quality groups. Children from higher social strata usually enter the "higher quality" groups and those from lower strata the "lower" ones. School decisions about a child's ability will greatly influence the kind and quality of education he receives, as well as his future life, including whether he goes to college, the jobs he will get, and his feelings about himself and others.

The chief official instruments used for sorting students into homogeneous or ability groups are standardized tests and teacher judgments. Unofficial factors often enter the selection decision—such as parental intervention, a child's behavior, or quotas in each grouping.

Important variables in the sorting process are permanence, type, and age of selection. In general the later the age of selecting students, and the more temporary and integrated the groupings created, the less stratification will be produced. For example children who are placed in low-ability groups in the first grade and segregated from others throughout the school day for six or eight years will be more firmly fixed in the lower strata of school and society than childen who attend classes with others for all or part of the day throughout their elementary school lives. Stratification has increased in American schools. The "tightening of standards" following Sputnik moved homogeneous grouping into early grades in a presumed effort to isolate the scientifically gifted. Transfer of Negroes out of segregated schools also pushed ability grouping downward into early grades as a means of separating the newcomers. Project Talent reports that 54 percent of high schools had homogeneous groupings and 49 percent had tracks in the early 1960's.

[21] *Equality of Educational Opportunity, op. cit.,* p. 21.
[22] Richard deNeufville and Caryl Connor, "How Good Are Our Schools: Armed Forces Qualifications Tests Provide a Clue," *American Education* (October, 1966), 2–9.

stratification: classrooms in a class society

Groupings range from temporary separation of ability groups within the same class to separation into different schools. They may apply to part of the day or the whole day; they may be temporary or permanent. Extreme forms of tracking, in which children are virtually assigned permanent classifications, can generate a self-fulfilling prophecy for both child and teacher of success or failure. Even Conant, concerned mainly about the "gifted," advised that "there should be no classification of students according to clearly defined and labeled programs or tracks such as 'college preparatory,' 'vocational,' 'commercial.' " [23] Grouping of elementary school children based on ability is prohibited as undemocratic in France and Scandinavia.

"We sound like the manager of a furniture factory," says Ernest Melby, "rejecting pieces of lumber in making tables." The school's "scrap heap," he says, comprises a third of the children. "Few manufacturing establishments could survive that large a scrap pile." [24] As for separating the gifted, Bruno Bettleheim says, "taking the gifted child out of the regular classroom and pushing him ahead as fast as he can move creates very serious problems for the child and for all society." [25] Benefits have been found in integrated classrooms and schools. Dr. Robert Cole found that the scholastic work of a group of Negro students bussed into a white school improved and that they became "brighter, more active, more alert, more eager to learn, more willing to work." [26] The Buchheimers found that the mixing of slow- and rapid-learning children, and white and Negro children, in one suburban school system, improved the performance of all the children.[27]

Part of the stratification process is the "normal curve of distribution," a statistical extrapolation that has been erroneously interpreted by some educators to mean that a certain proportion of students must be "failures," another percentage "near misses," and on up to "honors." Such categories are arbitrary labels assigned, not by statistics, but by the stratification process in the schools. On a test suitably constructed for the purpose, *even the gifted* will distribute themselves rather evenly around a mean and form a "normal curve"; those at the bottom however could scarcely be termed failures, though that is the usual label used in student rankings.

Most upper-income parents do not tolerate a system in which administrators expect that teachers will grade on a curve, from honors to failure. The common assumption that 10 or 20 percent of students must fail according to the iron laws of statistics and the demands of secondary and higher education and that students must thereby be ranked and only a certain proportion given "A's," "B's," etc., is more than suspect as a means of educating and dealing justly with students.

IQ and Culture

Evidences of applied psychology in the schools are intelligence testing and the concept of "cultural deprivation." Both have been

[23] In late 1965, massive protests of Washington, D. C. civil rights groups focused on that city's tracking system (honors, college prep, regular, and basic); as a result 800 pupils wrongly placed in the "basic" track for mentally subnormal were put into regular tracks. James B. Conant, *The American High School* (New York: McGraw-Hill, 1959).

[24] Ernest O. Melby, "The Deprived Child: His Gift to Education," *The Disadvantaged*, Mott Institute for Community Improvement, College of Education, Michigan State University (June, 1966), 1:4.

[25] Bruno Bettleheim, "Stop Pampering Gifted Children," *Saturday Evening Post*, April 11, 1964.

[26] Report on a study of Dr. Robert Cole in *Education Summary*, May 1, 1966.

[27] Arnold and Naomi Buchheimer, "Equality Through Integration," ADL of B'nai B'rith, pamphlet.

stratification: classrooms in a class society

popular alternatives to the hypothesis that the *school* is the primary source of stratified achievement and failure among low-income children. One contributed the thesis that the "limited native *intelligence*" of the disadvantaged was the prime source of failure, and the other that family life and *group* culture was responsible.

"Nowhere in the world," says Martin Mayer, "except in Britain, does the IQ score influence people's expectations of a child so greatly as it does in the United States. The French will not have such tests given to normal elementary school children, under any circumstances, before the last year of the primary program." [28] IQ tests, critics claim, are biased in favor of the language and training of upper-strata children and do not measure native ability. They further claim that these tests label students, retard the progress of many, and provide a rationale for the failure of schools. It is also said that they do not even attempt to measure creative ability, motivation, curiosity, persistence, industry, and capacity for sustained effort.

The tests have been eliminated in some city systems in favor of achievement tests which at least do not suggest genetic deficiencies in the child. [29] IQ tests are still used at the highest administrative levels however, as an explanation and justification of low pupil achievement, and it is still generally believed that IQ tests *do* measure native aptitude and that they are useful in sorting students.

Project Talent, the largest national survey of high school "talent" reported that students in slum areas make low achievement scores; "however, their relative average achievement in English and mathematics is just as high as that of students in the other large city schools when achievement level is adjusted for non-verbal scholastic aptitude as measured by the abstract reasoning test." Analysis *"shows no underperformance as relative to abstract reasoning ability."* [my italics]

The report then shifts to environment: "It would appear that such talent as the poor quality environment permits to emerge *may be adequately developed by the schools in our large cities.* If true, this is a *tribute to the strenuous efforts of our large city school administrations to equalize opportunity in all of their schools regardless of location."* [my italics]

Project Talent, its operations heavily influenced by school administrators, acknowledges no responsibility on the part of the school for the vast talent loss among the disadvantaged. [30]

THE CULTURE. As for "cultural deprivation," the total impression transmitted to many educators by the concept is that the "rejected," "disadvantaged," or "deprived" child is handicapped, not by school or society, but by their own culture and behavior, and that he is so different and "crippled" that he cannot be expected to achieve as others do. Many educators point to the culture of the child and family as a total explanation of school failure, but they do not, as an outcome of this belief, assume responsibility for changing that culture by extending the school into the community or bringing the family and community into the school.

Lower strata, and particularly Negro culture, are said by the "deprivationists" to be characterized by: authoritarian and strict child-rearing practices, matriarchical family and absence of father figure, much greater sexual free-

[28] Martin Mayer, *The Schools, op. cit.,* p. 98.
[29] Joseph O. Loretan, "The Decline and Fall of Group Intelligence Testing," *Teachers College Record* (October, 1965), 67:1.
[30] Project Talent, *op. cit.*

dom, family instability, illegitimacy, impulse gratification, more physical in general orientation, parent-child ties more casual and custodial, slow reactions, general language deficiencies. The language of lower strata youth, in Britain and elsewhere, is said to provide them with a "relatively low level of conceptualization" and a "low order of causality" compared to middle-class youth; they also rely more on non-verbal techniques such as "gesture, volume and tone of voice, facial expression, and physical set." [31]

"Generally, the culture of the lower classes is simple and more primitive," says Egon Bergel. "It can produce short songs, dances, stories, small paintings, and little sculptures. It lacks the ability to create epics, novels, dramas, symphonies, monumental sculptures, or great paintings. In sciences the lower classes are absolutely sterile. As a whole their culture reflects a lower level of intellectual and psychological development. The other classes are fully mature and their cultures are more elaborate, more sophisticated, more complex, more mature." Conversely, he continues, "the uppermost stratum is more remote from nature, least vigorous, and in the greatest danger of becoming decadent. . . ." [32] The upper strata in contrast to the lower are composed of "persons possessed of strong ambitions, bold and adventurous characters, with inventive minds, with harsh and non-sentimental characters . . . and . . . with a will for domination and power." [33]

Frank Riessman has summarized some of the *positives* of "deprived" culture including directness, simplicity, activity, spontaneity. [34]

Many cultural differences, however significant they may be to school achievement, are adaptive responses to social realities and inequities, and are hardly under the unaided control of the family culture.

Some researchers have written about the "inability of working class children to postpone gratification"—their unwillingness, for example, to refuse full-time jobs that will return immediate rewards in favor of continuance in school. What is not discussed is that the child's value system has been validated by experience and that the child is not likely to learn in a setting where he is asked to abandon what in his experience can guarantee his survival. If he is to survive, he quickly learns to seize the chance before him. In his experience, to defer a gratification is to deny it. A system of rewards—especially material rewards—is beyond his imagination, for no one he knows has the means to reward him. If he saves, he probably will be forced to yield up the savings to help his family through one of the recurrent crises it faces. If he does not eat what is put before him, when it is offered, a hungry brother or parent will. He has never heard of anyone who "made it" socially in economic competition. He has learned that competition leads to extinction. If he does not stick with the gang, he is assaulted by other gangs. If he humiliates his fellows by always excelling he is excluded from their company, isolated, threatened. If he is a Negro or Latin, he knows that the world is hostile and that his only defense is in the group. The teacher who tries to make him compete against the group in the usual way exposes himself as an enemy who would steal his security.

Psychologists who stress family culture have also emphasized the preschool and early years as formative for the child. This view is based on ob-

[31] Basil Bernstein, "Some Sociological Determinants of Perception: An Inquiry into Sub-Cultural Differences," *The British Journal of Sociology* (1958), 159–179.

[32] Egon E. Bergel, *Social Stratification* (New York: McGraw-Hill, 1962), p. 431.

[33] Pitirim A. Sorokin, *Social and Cultural Mobility* (Glencoe: The Free Press, 1959), p. 308.

[34] Frank Riessman, *The Culturally Deprived Child* (New York: Harper, 1962).

servation of stability of personality and achievement of children continuing into adulthood—rather than on evidence about the relative effects of influencing child behavior at *various* ages, from infancy to adulthood. "The power of early learning must still, for humans, remain largely an inference from theory," says Benjamin Bloom.[35] Persuasive longitudinal studies on the effect of preschool education on later performance are lacking and some contrary evidence points to the repeated finding that the "deprived" enter kindergarten as the intellectual equal of other children but regress steadily as they continue in school, starting in about the third or fourth grade. This would tend to indicate that the problem is in the school rather than the preschool years spent at home.

A neglected postulate concerning the decline in achievement is that the "deprived child" often learns by contact with life outside his home, in school and society, that he and his group are "rejected," that they have little power over rules and conditions that govern their lives, and that, based on this awareness, the child may respond as early as the third grade by silent or open resistance and resentment. Also, in the third grade the child advances into a struggle with the written word of an unusually difficult language, all the more troublesome for those disadvantaged to whom it is not altogether native.

The term "cultural deprivation," says Kenneth Clark, masks the fact that these are human beings who are "deliberately and chronically victimized by the larger society in general, and by educational institutions specifically." He suggests that one of the things we should do "is get rid of our guilt-determined sentimentalism and over-solicitousness in the actual education process. Let us approach these children in terms of educational requirements, standards, and demands, as if they were human beings and not lepers. Let us not teach these children as if they were different, as if one had to be specifically careful how you teach them to read." [36]

The doctor-patient relationship is not present in the school. If a patient is sick and does not get well, it is assumed that the doctor or the state of medical knowledge has failed. The patient or his family culture is rarely blamed; nor is the patient told to leave the hospital because he refused to get well. The school, on the other hand, often assumes that the child, or his parents, have failed and that this is a normal feature of statistical law. Educators who assume that one out of ten or so must fail are surprised when they meet resistance or rebellion. Doctors who assumed that one out of ten must die on the operating table might arouse similar responses in patients. It would be equally foolish of course, for doctors to assume that there were *no* differences between their patients and the normal population. Their patients are sick and the doctor's job is to cure them.

Perhaps the most striking attributes of the disadvantaged that need positive attention in the school are: a sense of powerlessness and a deficiency of middle class verbal skill.

The sense of impotence among American Negroes has derived largely from a deficiency of power in both political and economic systems, power usually provided by votes and jobs. In the schools, they have often been separated from the majority, and deprived of equal educational opportunity. (Even in Northern cities where Negroes have greatest political and economic power, they have held few positions of power in the schools.) Feelings of powerless-

[35] Benjamin S. Bloom, *Stability and Change in Human Characteristics* (New York: John Wiley, 1965), p. 216.
[36] Kenneth Clark, "The Clash of Cultures in the Classroom," *Integrated Education*, 1963.

ness among the disadvantaged, says Melvin Seeman, inhibit knowledge.[37] Hospital patients who feel powerlessness, he points out know less about health matters than those who do not. Unorganized workers were similarly found to feel more powerless than the organized—and the greater the personal involvement in union affairs, the less was the sense of impotence. A person's feelings of self-reliance and power, he concludes, are tied up with whether he belongs to an organization that has some control over his occupational destiny, and the more active in these organizations he is the greater his sense of power. It is out of the need for power and for a "sense of power" that peer group, gang life, and collective behavior acquire such a strong hold over low income youth.

The largest survey in American education, *Equality of Educational Opportunity*, reported that verbal fluency of students was more closely linked to a sense of power than any other variable related to achievement.[38]

Verbal skill, which is highly correlated with almost all forms of school achievement, presents special problems for those disadvantaged who speak a variant of the English language. This handicap requires that schools emphasize verbal skills more strongly, find new methods of teaching "middle-class" English (perhaps as a second language), and discover ways to prevent cleavage between home and school when different dialects are used.

Achievement and Its Correlates

As we have seen, the society stratifies its members and offers to various strata widely variant material and status rewards. The school is part of the society's stratification system to the extent that it prepare students (consciously or out of habit) for a "place" in society like that occupied by their parents.

To more effectively pursue the goal of equal educational opportunity, it appears that schools must turn attention to:

Community. Community education to help people organize to gain power in the political and economic systems, share power in the school system and participate in various school roles, change community attitudes to a "real" sense of mastery of the environment.

Higher education. Use the influence of school and community to open opportunities in higher education and qualify students for college admission.

Attitudes. Convince teachers and administrators that disadvantaged children can, with proper attention, achieve as others do.

Equality. Imaginative compensatory programs to make up for past and present inequalities in the schools.

Segregation. Limit the separation of students, within and between schools, based on class, ethnic, or ability factors.

Methods. Devise improved methods of teaching verbal skills, and integrating instruction with the events of the real world.

Personnel. Use new types of personnel in newly defined non-professional and other roles.

Some national studies have tried to discover what variables are most highly correlated with achievement and what schools can most effectively do to raise achievement. These and other efforts have been inconclusive. Project Talent reported tentatively that two factors significantly correlated with achieve-

[37] Melvin Seeman, "Antidote to Alienation—Learning to Belong," *Trans-action* (May–June, 1966), 3:4.
[38] *Equality of Educational Opportunity, op. cit.*

ment were teacher salaries, and the amount of money spent in school districts, holding socioeconomic factors constant. *Equality of Educational Opportunity*, a report financed by $1 million from the United States Office of Education, tentatively reported that *class* integration of students, quality of teachers, and—also tentatively—the student's sense of mastery accounted for more of the variance in performance on verbal skills tests than did differences between school facilities and offerings. The study, in fact, reports a between-school variance of Southern Negro students in the third grade, a critical year, as 34.68. It also reports that the disadvantage to twelfth grade Negroes of going to school in the rural South as contrasted with the urban North is 30 percentile points in the distribution of scores. Twelfth grade Negroes in the urban Northeast were 2.9 grades behind that of whites in the urban Northeast, but in the rural South they were 4.9 grades behind.[39] The report mainly concerns itself with demonstrating that variance *within* schools is greater than variance *between* schools and that inequalities between schools, therefore, make little difference.

Of course, great variance always exists among individuals within any given group and is usually far greater than the *average* difference between groups. Variance *within* schools seems less pertinent to the education of the disadvantaged than the questions: Do school inequalities in expenditures, quality, and attitudes of teachers and administrators, power arrangements, facilities and curriculum, or opportunities in higher education make a significant difference to student achievement? What can schools do—or what have they done to significantly improve performance?

In the St. Louis schools, Negro administrator Samuel Sheppard was able to significantly raise achievement by emphasizing learning, working with parents, and changing administrator and teacher attitudes and introducing better incentives to achievement.

Earned Rewards

In the United States status and rewards can be earned by ability and effort, but they seem earned more often by parental status and know-how about how to acquire status: marking time in educational institutions in order to "qualify" for the degree elite and a cluster of factors that relate to "striving." These include: a manipulative attitude toward rules, people, institutions; a thick skin to the criticism and failure that discourage many people; insistent demand on the part of individuals and groups for better treatment; group organization that seeks rewards for insiders and excludes outsiders.[40]

Status in schools and society often derives from membership in organized ethnic groups. At the top of the ethnic hierarchy and the power elite in the society has been the white Anglo-Saxon Protestant, the first and largest immigrant group, one possessing the advantage of initial mastery of both the language and the land of the New World. All American Presidents (except John F. Kennedy) and Vice-presidents have been WASP, as have most high-ranking officials, heads of educational institutions and large corporations. The record of stratification in the United States marks the slow ascent of the ethnic and religious minorities—Jewish (3 percent of the population over 14 years of age); Roman Catholic (26 percent of the population)—and now Negro Protestants (9 percent)—into some positions of status and influence in American schools and society.

[39] *Equalizing Educational Opportunity, op. cit.*
[40] About half of the top executives of the 600 largest United States non-financial corporations have fathers who were also either heads of the same corporation or independent businessmen.

63

With economic expansion, upward mobility has increased and many people have entered higher income brackets. In 1962, 19 percent of American families had incomes of $10,000 or more; in 1929, the figure was five percent (in terms of 1962 dollars); and in 1947, nine percent. During the second World War, the share of wealth owned by top groups declined and that of bottom groups increased. Since the war, the share of the bottom 20 percent has declined somewhat. The share of the upper 30 percent has increased, and there has been greater concentration of income in the upper middle-income groups.

According to Rogoff, mobility rates in the United States have not changed much during the first half of the 20th century.[41] The United States rate and that of the U.S.S.R. have been high compared to other nations, but the U.S.S.R. also has a high downward mobility rate, indicating that people fall as well as rise in status.[42]

An individual's position in the stratification hierarchy, which is greatly influenced by school experiences, affects almost all aspects of his life. In general, the higher the position the more money he will have, the greater will be his prestige and authority, the better his housing and health, the less dangerous his neighborhood, the more extensive his vacations, the better his food and clothes, the greater his security, freedom, and privacy, and the more interesting his job.

The standardized mortality ratios of unskilled workers in 1950 was 120; skilled workers 96, professionals 82.[43] As for mental illness, one study showed that about 5 percent of the lower strata, 21 percent of the middle, and 47 percent of the higher strata with neuroses received therapeutic treatment.[44] After 15 or more years of marriage, 50 to 60 percent of the lower strata, but only 15 percent of upper-middle class families were broken through separation, desertion, divorce or death.[45] Thirty percent of unskilled workers reported no close friends; 13 percent of skilled, small business, and white-collar workers; and 10 percent of professionals, top business, and officials.[46] Average life-time travel reported by lower strata was a radius of 145 miles, by higher strata, 1,100.[47]

In general, the more education one gets, the higher will be one's place in the stratification hierarchy. Sixty-two percent of people with a grade school education voted, 80 percent with a high school education, 90 percent of those with college education.[48]

[41] Natalie Rogoff, "Recent Trends in Urban Mobility," in P. K. Hatt and Albert Reiss (eds.), *Reader in Urban Sociology* (Glencoe: The Free Press, 1951), pp. 406–420.

[42] S. M. Miller, "Comparative Social Mobility," *Current Sociology* (1960), 9:56.

[43] L. Guralnick, "The Study of Mortality by Occupation in the United States" (Washington, D. C.: National Office of Vital Statistics, September, 1959).

[44] A. Hollingshead and J. Redlich, *Social Class and Mental Illness* (New York: Wiley, 1958), based on Table 26, p. 267.

[45] August B. Hollingshead, "Class Differences in Family Stability," *Annals* of the American Academy of Political and Social Science (November, 1950), 39–46.

[46] Joseph A. Kahl, *The American Class Structure* (New York: Rinehart, 1957), pp. 137–138.

[47] J. Useem, P. Tangent, and R. Useem, "Stratification in a Prairie Town," *American Sociological Review* (1942), 7:331–342.

[48] Robert E. Lane, *Political Life* (Glencoe: The Free Press, 1959), pp. 48–49.

stratification: classrooms in a class society

organization
and bureaucracy
six

The school, as a social institution, is a large-scale organization involved, as are industry, the military, and other groups, in the management of vast institutions. The health of the school depends on the ability of its managers to organize it successfully. Similarly, the health of other institutions and of the society itself is closely tied to administrative skills. The United States has been fortunately endowed with an abundance of organizational ability. Such skill, running from bottom to top in the society, has often been called the peculiar American genius. Certainly our national development has been closely linked to our skill in forming and running effective organizations.

Administrators occupy a strategic role in the school organization and greatly influence what transpires in the classroom. In the school, however, interest in and capacity for organization have been relatively scarce. Of fifteen standard textbooks on school administration selected at random, Daniel E. Griffiths found not a single source which devoted as much as a full chapter to organization, or the definition of duties, responsibilities, power, and authority.[1] This has definitely not been the case, he says, in the literature of business and public administration.

The classroom is a subsystem of the school, a dependent part of the whole. Decisions made by administrators of an organization determine the method

[1] Daniel E. Griffiths, et al., *Organizing the Schools for Effective Education* (Danville, Ill.: The Interstate Printers and Publishers, 1962), p. 3.

and content of classroom instruction, the size of the class, the goals of the organization, the characteristics of the classroom teachers, the hierarchy of personnel, the stratification of the students, and the degree of school-community interaction. Decisions made at the top can even abolish the classroom and establish alternative patterns of organization, such as independent or group study, tutorials, or mass media instruction, none of which need a traditional classroom. Such decisions could conceivably abolish teachers, change their functions, or otherwise dramatically alter the mode of instruction.

Educational research has usually concentrated on what transpires inside the traditional classroom and ignored the larger organizational context. Similarly, criticisms directed at classroom teachers by many parents indicate that they regard the classroom as the ultimate unit of authority in the school. It is as though, in warfare, the "enemy" and the "foot soldiers" were equated and the invisible target, a complex military establishment operating far behind the front line, ignored.

The major organizational problems of the school today are concerned with authority, efficiency, and with integration of the school with other parts of the social system.

Integration of Systems

Schools, more than most organizations, perform functions that are an integral part of the whole social system. They produce not nuts and bolts for a specified market, but children who eventually should participate fully in the various economic, political, educational, familial, and other institutions of the society. It is the school's task to improve that participation. Yet the schools seem more detached from the social system than other constituent parts. In the recruitment of personnel, for example, the schools are quite ingrown and isolated. Although people with varied experience and training can rise to executive positions in government and private industry, the schools select administrators almost exclusively from within their own ranks. The business executive may be trained in philosophy, geology, or simply hard knocks, but the school administrator must be trained in teaching and school administration. When a bureaucracy is large and powerful, as in city systems, not only is training narrowly prescribed, but pressures often demand the promotion only of those trained and experienced in the *same system*. While this provides continuity and opportunity within the system, it also shields it from encounters with fresh ideas and people introduced from outside. It has, in short, the qualities of incestuous breeding.

Not only is the circle from which administrators and teachers are selected narrowly drawn, the school itself, and the children in it, exist in virtual isolation from the society. Except for limited work-study programs, students acquire no intimate knowledge of business, financial, labor, or governmental institutions. Students are shielded from genuine political debate and involvement by the morality and nonpartisan structure of the school. Even contacts with the intellectual, cultural, and religious life of their own and other societies is limited.

Among the urgent reasons for educational sociology to enter the mainstream of general sociology is the contribution which analyses of other large-scale organizations can make toward improving the operation of educational organizations.

Order and Change

Institutions carry on two simultaneous functions: (1) preserving order in the society by moderating violence and conflict, and (2)

organization and bureaucracy

responding to changes and new social needs. Because of their hierarchical nature, chain of command, and general complexity, most institutions are less accessible to influence from lower than from upper social strata. School systems, more hierarchical than many bureaucracies, seem less responsive to influence from below than other organizations.

The survival chances of a society, says Robert Presthus, "are largely a function of its ability to meet change." When they do not "harness their values and institutions to the demands of social, economic and climatic change, civilizations have rapidly declined." [2] A characteristic of large organizations, he adds, is "their inflexibility in the face of social and technological pressures for change." [3]

Authority

As organizations have grown in size, the bureaucracies of administrators who run them—corporate, public, military, educational—have become a target of widespread criticism. Bureaucracy has been portrayed as a vast, impersonal system of rules, file numbers, and forms—run by stolid administrators and unresponsive to individual needs, deviation, or public demand for change.

As analyzed by Max Weber, modern bureaucracy is not a villain but is, on the contrary, a more efficient manager than older systems which were often run by people who inherited rather than earned their positions. Characteristics of bureaucracy, Etzioni points out are: (1) rules and regulations that facilitate standardization and equality in the handling of individual cases; (2) systematic division of labor, rights, and power; (3) a hierarchy of offices; (4) authority based on knowledge and ability rather than inherited position; (5) administration separated from ownership; (6) freedom from outside control of monopoly; (7) rules and records embodied in written rather than oral communication.[4] Presthus adds that most big organizations are characterized by specialization, status anxiety, oligarchy (rule by the few), co-optation (selection of their successors by the organization's elite), efficiency, and rationality.[5] On many of these counts some large city school systems would qualify as "ideal bureaucracies." Still, these systems may be seen as much less than "ideal" in their efficiency, the satisfaction they offer participants, and their responsiveness to social change. Rules are no doubt preferable to whim or favoritism in governing organizations. It is their appropriateness and flexibility which gives rise to complaints.

Goals and Authority

Profitmaking organizations have a clear goal: make as much money as possible. Many religious organizations have clear missions: serve God and instruct members. School goals are more ambiguous. The primary function of schools has been to teach various skills and knowledge. This task is complicated by other, sometimes conflicting, tasks. One is to relate the child to the society's authority system. Training the young in skills and knowledge is greatly simplified, in a sense, when the teacher is accepted as an unquestioned

[2] Robert Presthus, *The Organizational Society* (New York: Alfred A. Knopf, 1962), p. 27.

[3] *Ibid.*, p. 291.

[4] Amitai Etzioni, *Modern Organizations* (Englewood Cliffs, N. J.: Prentice-Hall, 1964), p. 53.

[5] Presthus, *op. cit.*, p. 27.

authority. But a democratic society is unclear about what its authority system should be. Spurred by social changes, our system has been moving away from coercive authority and toward voluntary and normative authority—toward a system where people submit not because they are forced to, but because they participate in making the rules, internalize the system's values, or use the system for "utilitarian" ends.

The sharpest philosophic debate in American education has concerned authority. In a democratic society, driven by the Protestant ethic, each man is assumed to be his own authority and government is presumed to rule by authority of the governed. While national *political* institutions often reflect this "ideal" authority system, *business* organizations tend to be more highly centralized, with decision-making residing in top bureaucracies.

Schools more nearly resemble the business than the political authority structure. Many public schools, nevertheless, have tried to relax coercive authority in order to train for democratic citizenship, just as the family has become more permissive in child rearing. It is often this effort, unmatched by successful techniques for promoting either "normative" or "utilitarian" authority, that causes schools to swerve from academic and other goals. Essentially a coercive system, it has tried to relax its rules without giving any real power over rule-making and enforcement to others in the system. In a word, it is the "discipline" problem in schools, one of the most serious and continuing problems of education—more extreme in the schools perhaps than in any other organization, including military and penal institutions. The student is taught (a) that in a democracy he is his own authority, (b) that the essential element of intellectual emancipation is the questioning of all authority. Yet he is denied any genuine authority in the conduct of institutions that govern his life. There is considerable doubt, says Etzioni, "whether the higher in rank can serve as leaders for the lower ranks in coercive organizations. Officials, it seems, must either reduce the coerciveness of the organization, or give up hope of effective formal leadership." [6]

Selection

The school authority problem is complicated by the lack of selectivity in recruitment. School is compulsory; all must attend. If public schools selected students as parochial schools and higher education do the discipline problem would almost vanish. Prisons reduce the discipline problem by giving significant authority to inmate organizations. Schools have created few alternatives for the large number of youth who resist present coercive adult authority. Such optional patterns are most urgently needed in the early teens when peer authority is strongest and adult authority weakest.

In the absence of an effective student movement, it may be speculated that as the power of educational institutions grows, particularly the university, the utilitarian authority of schools will increase and the "undisciplined" will learn to submit in order to cash in on the diploma. It is not clear that such an attack on nonconformity will have an altogether agreeable effect on schools or society. Students and schools will be made more governable, but healthy protest and adaptability to change may also be casualties. Schools and other big organizations enlist anxiety and deference toward authority in the service of their goals—responses which, in exaggeration, may be even more undesirable in the schools and less functional to the organization than excesses of disorder and assertiveness.

[6] Etzioni, *op. cit.*, p. 62.

68

Centralization

Successful organizations have varying patterns of command and authority. General Motors is so decentralized that its various units are competitive and almost autonomous. The Roman Catholic Church, at the other extreme, has been highly centralized. Both are successful large-scale organizations. Authority in public schools is relatively centralized. In large cities, operating centralized schools is such a management strain that in New York City, for example, as many administrators are employed to perform the job as in all the schools of France. To meet demands for more responsive policies, some large systems have tried to decentralize authority to district administrators and lay boards, and even to individual schools.

In general, the American ideal of local lay control of schools has not been realized in the city, where the centers of top authority have been remote from the individual school. Some decentralization to individual or district schools has occurred but the GM practice of making these autonomous units in order to increase efficiency has never been followed. Such administrative shuffling of authority as has occurred has often resulted in confusion and buck-passing between top- and middle-management, making it even more difficult for consumers (parents and students) to hold these organizations accountable. Organizations may be listed on a continuum of control by consumers, the public schools and universities being among those with least consumer control.

Shifts to lower management levels, according to Ernest Dale, have these advantages for organizations: (1) The people concerned are those making the decisions. Since they often know more about the factors affecting the decision, they may be able to make better and faster decisions. (2) The expense in money and time of central coordination is reduced. (3) The opportunity for those further down the organizational hierarchy to assume responsibility and act creatively may improve the quality of work all along the line.[7] Disadvantages are: (1) lack of uniformity of decisions; (2) failure to use the advice of specialists who would be more available to a centralized organization; (3) duplication of effort; (4) difficulty of executives to accept decentralization. The latter is traced to tradition and one-man direction, the expense of wrong decisions and duplication of effort, the seeming loss of power and prestige.[8]

Daniel Griffiths' view is that the less centralization, "the more effective will be the decision-making process . . . the more responsive will be the formal organization structure to changes suggested by the development of informal patterns of operation."[9]

In many countries a federal system of higher education has resulted in over-centralization, according to sociologist Joseph Ben-David, and a deficiency of regional initiative. French academies, he points out, were centralized by Napoleon into a unified academic system, situated mainly in Paris. The German system, on the other hand, was decentralized by the political dismemberment of Germany into 19 independent universities. This decentralization, he says, may have made the difference in the scientific creativity of the two countries. In Germany it gave rise to academic competition, which forced upon the individual institutions changes which would otherwise not have been

[7] Ernest Dale, *Planning and Developing the Company Organization Structure* (New York: American Management Association, 1955), p. 112.
[8] *Ibid.*, pp. 112–113, 118–119.
[9] Griffiths, *op. cit.*, p. 59.

made. In all cases crucial to the development of the medical sciences, he notes, German policies turned out to be more farsighted and bolder than the French.[10]

As for the effect of decentralizing power to faculty and students, Seymour Harris says, "I have been very much impressed with the inefficiencies of universities and colleges generally. The explanation, I believe, is in part that the college is run, to a considerable extent by the faculty." He reasons that where there are "so many who determine policy, obviously the result is not likely to be so good as in private enterprise."[11] It can be said on the other side that in the United States faculty has very little administrative authority and even where it has *none*, institutions are not run with notable efficiency. Perhaps the problem lies more in the capacities of educational administrators than in the authority of their faculties.

Human Relations and Scientific Management

During the first several decades of the twentieth century, the emphasis in educational administration was on scientific management. "It reflected," says L. Urwick, "the efficiency-engineering movement in industry and the scientific movement in education. . . . Emphasis was on organizational structure and the formal relationships of personnel to obtain efficiency in operation."[12]

Informal organization was largely ignored, resulting in an "authoritarian type of administration where major stress was put upon the organization's goals and little attention was given to the personal needs and dispositions of the organization members."[13] The school evaluation survey conducted by outside experts became a popular expression of the new scientific management emphasis.

This classical approach to administration—the search for more efficient and effective organization—did not noticeably raise the level of school efficiency, perhaps because administrators were, in fact, preoccupied with the most routine aspects of management.

The human relations approach to management, deriving from psychologists Elton Mayo, Kurt Lewin, and others, and emphasizing the needs of employees, did not become very influential in the schools until, as in industry, the unionization of employees called attention to human needs. Critics claimed that human relations became a manipulative device for controlling unionization and persuading employees to tolerate conditions which were essentially contrary to their interests.

The organization, Presthus says, fosters several personality types, among them: upward-mobiles, indifferents, and ambivalents. ". . . most organization men are indifferents. Alienated to some extent by work and the work place, they have displaced their energy and their interest upon off-work activities. Even the upward-mobile, whose élan remains high, seems less interested in the intrinsic value of work than in its by-products of authority, status, and prestige. If meaningful work is essential to mental health, the human consequences of such orientations are disturbing."[14] If we can "abandon some of our pragmatic notions about 'efficiency,' humanistic values will benefit, and the need for a

[10] Joseph Ben-David, "Scientific Productivity and Academic Organization in Nineteenth-Century Medicine," *American Sociological Review* (December, 1960), 25:828–843.

[11] Seymour Harris, *Challenge and Change, op. cit.,* p. 23.

[12] L. Urwick, *The Elements of Administration* (New York: Harper, 1944), p. 132.

[13] *Encyclopedia of Educational Research*, 3rd ed., a project of the American Educational Research Association, a department of the NEA (New York: Macmillan, 1960), p. 2.

[14] Presthus, *op. cit.,* p. 323.

70

organization and bureaucracy

permissive work climate in creative areas may become clearer." [15] Authority and status anxiety are antagonistic to individual self realization, which is all important. "No competent research exists demonstrating the 'efficiency' of the bureaucratic model compared with some alternative."

In the schools, administrative oligarchy and authority create dissatisfaction. The distress, however, seems to be caused by organization *inefficiency* rather than efficiency. In fact, the schools excel neither in human relations nor efficiency. Greater organizational efficiency might decentralize power to consumers and make individual schools more autonomous and competitive. Teachers might have clearer and more manageable roles; learning might be more voluntary and stimulating; and more personal attention might be given the child.

Communication and Feedback

Large-scale organization was facilitated by new communications technology. In particular the telephone and airplane made it possible for widely dispersed people in an organization to be in instant contact with one another. The communication problem is a leading theme in modern literature because a complex society, undergoing rapid change, depends on an elaborate network of oral and written exchanges. The teaching-learning process itself is conducted largely by written and oral communication. To trace the communications flow in an organization is to trace the organization's lifeline. Who calls, writes, talks to, or meets with whom—formally or informally, during or after hours? Some organizations encourage two-way communication—from the top down and from the bottom up, and some encourage lateral exchanges among colleagues. Thus the "meeting" has become a symbol of organization life, and the telephone the tool of the organization man's trade.

Among the participants in the school's communication system, which is almost unexplored, are lay boards, private and government groups, schools of education, administration, education organizations, teachers, students, parents. The more obvious communication deficiencies have been: between central administration and lower administration, among teachers, from students to those above, between low-income parents and all school personnel.

Teachers within a school, and especially between schools, have little opportunity, though considerable need, for informal or formal communications. In most organizations a professional who has a problem may walk into a colleague's office or call him on the phone for immediate consultation. The teacher is an isolated captive in the classroom, unable to leave the room or use the phone, who must usually try to solve all problems on the spot without consultation.

Low-income parents, in comparison to upper-income parents, are out of touch with the school. Communications between schools, even "feeding" schools, are rare. Informal communications among students, of course, are so energetically conducted that it becomes a primary function of the school to inhibit them. The school telephone usually cannot be used even by the teaching staff. Written messages, a major bureaucratic tool, are sent to teachers by administrators and they in turn send some memos to parents, but the flow is seldom reversed.

Most organizations have difficulty getting feedback into the system in the form of honest communications from participants, but schools seem to have more than the usual problems. This communication obstruction often results in energetic bursts of exchange between citizens and schools. It has its most serious consequence in organizational inertia and atrophy.

[15] *Ibid.*, p. 323.

PUBLIC REVIEW. Related to communications deficiencies is the lack of clear channels for the management of conflict among school participants. There is no equivalent, for example, of the police review board or the ombudsman, people outside the system who mediate conflict within it; nor is there any structured grievance procedure, except for unionized teachers. Students and parents have almost no recourse to review of grievances by impartial bodies.

APPEALS SYSTEM. Appeals systems or internal judicial systems, through which members can institute action against organization officials, are present in some large organizations. IBM, instead of a union grievance procedure, uses an Open Door Policy of appeal that starts with the immediate superior and ends with the Chairman of the Board.[16] The Catholic Church has "recourses" from a decision of an administrative superior, directed to the Pope. The federal government's grievance procedure goes to the Civil Service Commission. The Army has a complaint system administered by the Inspector General. The United Auto Workers Union expends unusual effort "to give persons a fair opportunity for defense against accusation *and* avenues of recourse in the event of unjust acts by the officialdom." [17]

While formal organizations exert a widening influence on the individual, "the legitimacy of authority within these organizations is being questioned," says William Scott.[18] The broad acceptance, he says, of devices such as participation, democratic leadership, and sensitivity training to make group members more aware of the responses of others, "is evidence that policy-makers believe that the unmodified structure of formal authority creates dangerous inequalities in the distribution of satisfactions to people in the organization. Dangerous to the extent that if changes in the motivational climate are not introduced, the behavior of the organization as a cooperative system will be impaired." [19] Much unresolved conflict in the schools can be traced to the absence of judicial and appeals systems.

Efficiency

Factors other than authority that influence the efficiency of school operations are: size, incentives, and competition.

SIZE. One of the clearest trends in the organization of American schools has been the consolidation of small districts into larger units. In 1930 there were about 150,000 one-room schools, in 1961 only about 15,000. In 1930 there were about 130,000 school districts, in 1960 only about 20,000. While the optimum size for industrial organizations has been carefully studied, similar attention has not been given to schools or school systems.

Indications are that as organization size increases, morale decreases. The size and impersonality of organizations, say Presthus, encourages anxiety. "Feelings of helplessness and of frustration occur as organizational power and demands checkmate the individual's claims for autonomy." [20] Large schools and

16 Thomas J. Watson, Jr., *A Business and its Beliefs: The Ideas That Helped Build IBM* (New York: McGraw-Hill, 1963).
17 William G. Scott, *The Management of Conflict, Appeal Systems in Organization* (Homewood, Ill.: Richard D. Irwin, 1965), p. 19.
18 *Ibid.*, p. 123.
19 *Ibid.*, p. 124.
20 Presthus, *op. cit.*, p. 17.

72

organization and bureaucracy

school systems also repress communication among participants and the expression of desire for change, coming up from the bottom.

As in other organizations, educational bureaucracies tend to expand their size and power to whatever limits are permitted. While it may be efficient and desirable to consolidate some facilities and classes, especially in secondary schools, simple enlargement of schools is of questionable value.

INCENTIVES. In business organizations the primary incentive to performance is monetary. Other incentives are status rewards, normative rewards (where loyalty to the organization is developed), and achievement for its own sake.

School incentives are unique. Monetary rewards are absent for students, except as much delayed gratifications in later life. Status rewards are most common, but they are effective only with those who *want* and can *get* status for academic achievement. For others, it is usually a negative incentive. Some students simply enjoy academic learning, but many others, endowed with a desire to learn, nevertheless find little of interest in school subjects.

Desire to be accepted by peers and live by group norms are powerful incentives for many students. Instead of turning such motivation to educational ends, the school often counterposes its own norms and authority *against* those of the peer group. When the norms of peers conflict with school norms, youths will often choose sides against the school.

In military organizations men are motivated to great effort and bravery by loyalty to and pride in small groups such as the platoon. The military group is small, primary, identifiable, mutually dependent, competitive with other groups, and always threatened from outside. In the school, group loyalty among peers often becomes a powerful anti-organization incentive as the school tries to put individuals in competition and as it fails to direct group loyalties toward academic goals.

COMPETITION. Public schools are distinct from most business, labor, religious, and voluntary organizations in that they are a monopoly producing an indispensable product which consumers are legally compelled to use. No yardsticks are available to measure the quality of the product or the efficiency of production. Few controls are present to support consumer demands for high quality, wide distribution, and low cost. The organizational principle on which American industrial productivity is presumably based—open competition—does not operate at all in the public schools, except in higher education during periods when students have many choices of colleges to attend.

Methods of promoting educational competition have been suggested, among them: (1) autonomy and competition among schools or groups of schools within the same system; (2) complete freedom of movement for students, and incentives to school personnel based on enrollments; (3) creation of competitive independent schools with either private or public funds; (4) tuition grants to students which they may use at the school of their choice, public or private; (5) expansion into educational activities of other public and private organizations, such as private industry, government programs (antipoverty, labor, welfare, etc.) to create competitive schools.[21]

Specialization and Standardization

Modern industrial organization is based on division of labor and standardization of organizational operations. These simplify jobs and

[21] Christopher Jencks, "Cultivating Greater Diversity," *The New Republic* (Fiftieth Anniversary Issue, 1965).

job training and permit the easy substitution of personnel on various jobs. Automobiles, once handmade by a few skilled craftsmen, are now assembled by thousands of workers performing small, specialized, simple tasks that require little training to master. Moreover, the assembled parts are standardized and turned out by machine to almost identical specifications.[22]

The "conformity" in our society against which a growing "bohemia" has revolted, probably stems mainly from the industrial standardization of workers and products which rejects all that is irregular and deviant. While this standardization has been a necessary part of industrialization, creating material abundance and leisure for genuine creativity, it has neglected the unique in human and material development, and fragmented work tasks into repetitive, and often meaningless jobs.

Schools stand about midway between the old craft and the new factory systems of production. Among their standardized and specialized parts are: the classroom—of standard size, time span, and specialized content; school personnel—of standard training, characteristics, and specialized assignments; differentiated and specialized subject matter; units of course credits; age grading; standardized tests and texts; promotion based on marks; standard curriculum, especially in elementary school; standard building plans.

These may not be the best units of standardization. The method and content of instruction is relatively unstandardized, and the teacher's work task difficult to learn and execute. The semester unit and course credits are inflexible and not necessarily the most rational, and the semi-standardized classroom permits little attention to unique individual needs.

Age grading, as a basic unit of standardization, was unknown until the mid-nineteenth century. By 1860 it had been introduced into most city systems, but not without nostalgia for the ungraded, and even the one-room school, or longing for a system in which children could proceed at their own speed, without respect to age or grade. The Dalton and Winnetka plans permitted children to move ahead at their own speed and were more successful than traditional programs in academic instruction. A strong trend toward non-graded early elemetary school has recently occurred.

Compared to industrial jobs, the classroom teacher's role is quite *un*defined and *un*standardized. Little is known about what tasks teachers actually perform or how much time is spent at them. Clearly, much time is consumed in clerical, disciplinary, and other tasks having no relation to instruction. When occupations are so ill-defined and unspecialized and when teaching materials and methods are similarly ambiguous or obsolete, the training of competent teachers becomes extremely difficult. Further specialization of these tasks, and the assignment of the simpler tasks to teacher aides, thereby creating a more graded hierarchy of school occupations, may produce a more efficient and successful organization. It would also produce clear career lines leading up from nonprofessional to professional jobs and create a better promotion and incentive system for school employees.

Technology

Schools have not yet been seriously touched by the new technology, although it is widely predicted that automation and standardization of routine parts of academic learning may greatly increase productivity.

Television, probably the most significant technological innovation since

[22] Harvey Pressman, "New Schools for the Poor, Designs for Equality and Excellence" (January, 1966), mimeographed.

organization and bureaucracy

the printing press, can reach out and communicate knowledge to voluntary learners, adults as well as children, in even the most backward rural areas. While American children watch TV as much as they attend school (about five hours a day), relatively little use is made of the media by schools.

Promotion and Public Relations

Transfer of knoweldge from the advertising industry might stimulate motivation and educational productivity if done with discretion. In a society of fiercely competing products, education also needs some selling. Such advertising might disseminate information about the value of education to personal and job satisfaction, along with specific knowledge about schools, and opportunities. Also, as publishers have learned, texts can, like other educational products, be attractively printed without vulgarization.

Financial and Performance Accountability

In many suburban school systems, annual accounts are sent to all citizens of money spent, personnel placements, programs and curriculums, student achievement records as compared to other systems, and so forth. In other systems such accounts may go only to school board members. To increase accountability it has been proposed that in large systems, each school issue such statements to those who pay for school services, the parents.

More adequate accounting *within* the organization is also needed. Martin Rein and S. M. Miller report that when a state department of mental hospitals began to send out monthly questionnaires to hospitals, asking for an account of the number of patients in straight-jackets, the number declined sharply each month—and similar improvements resulted when the employment service was asked to report referrals of Negroes to jobs.[23]

Accountability will undoubtedly be greatly facilitated by the application of computer technology to relevant information about the schools.

Management Efficiency

Any organization that wants to prevent organizational dry rot, says John W. Gardner, should provide the following: (1) effective programs for recruiting and developing talented employees; (2) a hospitable environment for individuals so that they will produce ideas and not feel like machine cogs; (3) clear channels for self-criticism; (4) fluidity of internal communications; (5) an adequate system of internal communications; (6) a fluid rather than rigid body of rules and regulations; (7) a means of combating the vested interests within the organization that prevent change; (8) an interest in what the organization is becoming rather than what it has been and a philosophy of innovation; (9) motivation, conviction, morale.[24]

Engaging outside consultants, encouraging internal criticism, bringing "new blood" into key posts, rotation of personnel are means he suggests for organizational renewal. "Americans," he observes, "have always been exceptionally gifted at organizational innovation. In fact, some observers say this is the true American inventiveness." [25] Such talent is clearly needed in the school.

[23] Martin Rein and S. M. Miller, "Social Action on the Installment Plan," *Trans-action* (January–February, 1966).

[24] John W. Gardner, "How to Prevent Organizational Dry Rot," *Harper's Magazine* (October, 1965), p. 22.

[25] Gardner, *op. cit.*, p. 26.

values
and ideology

seven

Values form the core of a society's culture and the typical values of the society form its norms. These values and norms are presumably taught by schools to the young through the *socialization* process, which shapes the behavior and personality of the individual.

Major institutions in a society may stress different and often conflicting values. The market may emphasize self-serving and acquisitive values—religion may stress charitable and altruistic values—and the family—group cohesion and happiness. Schools presumably extract the norms of the whole society for transmission to the young, but, in fact, school values represent a rather narrow band in the spectrum of social norms.

Values and culture tend to be more standard in middle-class than in lower-income families, simply because the former are more likely to be exposed and held to a common standard while considerable ethnic and cultural differences will be found in the latter. Values taught in school tend to be those of the middle class. Value conflicts among school, family, and peers cause great stress in the young and are the source of many school problems.

Education has become one of the highest-ranking American values. It is valued for its contribution to personal growth and self-improvement, for its use in getting a good job, and for its uses in social, scientific and technological development.

76

Achievement

A Value System

Though obituaries have announced the death of ideology, the United States is not without a value system. Central to that system is *achievement*. The individual must achieve his goals, succeed in school and on the job, and win the rewards of status, money, and friends. The rewards are often less important than the pursuit, and one plays to win as well as to collect the trophy. Achievement as an end in itself is partly a product of the school practice of offering no immediate material rewards but stimulating achievement for its own sake.

Achievement provides meaning and purpose for much of the population and makes the society successfully competitive with others. It is related to a whole system of values, including materialism, hard work, action, speed, efficiency, individualism, practicality, problem-solving, competition, aggression, mastery, risk-taking, adaptability, getting "results," good personal relations, team-work, voluntarism, optimism.

Also axiomatic in the value system is the belief that all people should have the same opportunities to achieve, a faith that all *can* achieve given a fair chance, and an indisposition to look too deeply into social inequities except under pressure from the disadvantaged in the system.

Achievement is circumscribed by strong sanctions in most groups against the "striver," the person who is so excessively driven to achievement that he steps on others, obeys even the most disagreeable rules, or otherwise violates peer codes. One must play by the rules, and those who do not, risk ostracism and public antipathy. Often the rules permit any amount of striving, as long as it does not "show"; hence students may indulge in secret studies and a show of nonchalance about school grades. Some sub-cultures strongly disapprove any "showing off" or ostentatious display of wealth, knowledge, or other trophies of achievement.

Though schools have been detached from the society, they have been solidly attached to the society's achievement values. Their inefficiency in teaching these values lies in the fact that scholastic achievement has not been directed at tangible material rewards or useful and practical activity. Instead students are expected to work and achieve without payment except in "honors."

Action and Utility

Few Americans, said Harold Laski, "find it easy to be happy unless they are doing something." [1] The man of action is the American hero—the Western cowboy, and the rare public figure such as President Kennedy. The hero is intelligent and "quick to figure things out," but not intellectual; he is concerned with immediate problems rather than theoretical issues. He "gets things done," useful things.

In developing areas a formidable obstacle to progress is inability of people to engage in action that produces quick results. In the United States, education has been neglected in public policy partly because it does not get fast results. Compared to many nations, there has been much criticism of traditional "book learning" as useless—too "academic," and unrelated to action or real problems. In Communist China, where traditional scholarship is unrelated to use and

[1] Harold Laski, *The American Democracy* (New York: Viking Press, 1948), p. 15.

action, Mao Tse-tung wrote, "reading a book is learning, but application is also learning and the more important form of learning. To learn warfare through warfare—this is our chief method."[2] It is learning by doing.

William James and John Dewey called it a "pragmatic" value system, freed of Old World dogmas, searching for what "works" without respect to dated rule books, judging outcomes by results rather than obedience to rules, preferring action to talk and the useful to style and good form.

The strictly academic has been valued in the United States usually only when its usefulness is clear to students. These uses may be self-serving (scholarship offers good jobs and other rewards) or society-serving (scholarship provides power and useful technology to the society).

Hard work and effort seem so habitual to Americans that they typically spend even leisure hours in action and do-it-yourself projects. In nations where manual labor is spurned by the privileged, Americans are noted for their readiness to "roll up their sleeves and go to work." Work was once a basic moral theme in the schools, as taught by McGuffey Readers in 1896: "Work, work, my boy, be not afraid; Look labor boldly in the face." The practical philosophy of Benjamin Franklin advised the young: "The way to wealth is as plain as the way to market. It depends chiefly on two works, industry and frugality; that is waste neither time nor money, but make the best use of both." Effort and hard work are still highly prized by the school.

The most striking contrast between United States schools and those abroad is that in our schools children more often do things, move about, talk, and engage in activity. The American preoccupation with doing is evident in the "activity curriculum," and the emphasis of some educators on learning by doing—both of which are seriously neglected in school practice.

Materialism

Americans share the apparently universal desire for the "good life" and money to purchase property, comfort, freedom, security, health, etc. Money to the American, said Santayana, "is the symbol and measure he has at hand for success, intelligence, and power; but as to money itself he makes, loses, spends and gives it away with a light heart."[3]

Richard Centers and Hadley Cantril found that two out of three people think that if they had more money they would be much happier.[4] A national poll showed that 31 percent of Americans identified their "biggest disappointment in life" as having to do with lack of money or with job dissatisfaction. The second most frequently identified disappointment was "lack of education" for self and children (22 percent).[5]

Despite the high value attached to money, 80 percent of high school students do not study economics and only 40 percent of high schools even offer a course in economics. Students learn neither about how to make money nor about the complicated economic system on which many national values are built.

[2] Mao Tse-tung, *Strategic Problems of China's Revolutionary War* (New York: Foreign Languages Press, 1954), p. 18.
[3] George Santayana, *Character and Opinion in the United States* (New York: George Braziller, 1920), p. 185.
[4] Richard Centers and Hadley Cantril, "Income Satisfaction and Income Aspiration," *Journal of Abnormal and Social Psychology* (January, 1946).
[5] A Lou Harris Survey, 1954.

Related Values

What counts in the "market" says H. Otto Dahlke, are "initiative, courage, conviction, perseverance of the individual." While hard work is valued, "the highest success will depend on the willingness to take a risk." [6] The American is typically guided by optimism. "The American knew," said Henry Steele Commager, "that nothing was impossible in his brave new world. . . . Progress was not, to him, a mere philosophical ideal but a commonplace of experience . . ." [7] An observer in Mexico reports, "The American believes all problems have a solution if you look hard enough and work hard enough; the Mexican lives in a hostile world that he feels he cannot control." [8]

In defining the five key social values, Florence Kluckhohn and Fred L. Strodtbeck assert that dominant American values hold that man is perfectible, capable of mastering nature, oriented to the future, oriented to active doing, and related to other men primarily as individuals. [9]

In contrast to these aggressive and active virtues, the schools' emphasis is on following directions, sitting still, being quiet, and passive rote learning rather than active problem solving.

The Achievement Society

The need for achievement, David C. McClelland asserts, "is the psychic capital of economic growth." He adds, "that Western business has developed by investing in the man rather than his plan." [10]

It is generally believed by economists that natural resources are important in economic growth but that what man makes of his environment is even more important. In Japan, for example, physical resources are scarce, but human resources are developed and Japan is an advanced nation. In other places, such as Brazil and Indonesia, physical resources are abundant but human resources neglected and the countries are relatively undeveloped.

The object of education in developing nations, says McClelland, should be to create entrepreneurial talent by developing the need for achievement, making better use of achievement resources, and increasing other-directedness (sociability and responsiveness to others). The psychologist's priorities, McClelland says, are for investing in improved communications, taking women out of the home, testing executives for achievement need, and reorienting teachers to a new kind of education that stresses group participation and achievement. Emancipation of women is necessary, he claims, because women carry the new culture to the next generation. Participation in school extra-curricular activities, he says, is an important way in which children learn to be responsive to the wishes of others and more other-directed. [11] Values associated with achievement need which the school should promote, are risk-taking, individual responsibility, knowledge of how to get results, delay of rewards. Child-rearing practices required to produce such values, he claims, are warmth, low father dominance (but not absence), and high achievement standards.

[6] H. Otto Dahlke, *Values in Culture and Classroom* (New York: Harper, 1958).
[7] Henry Steele Commager, *America in Perspective* (New York: Random House, 1947).
[8] Alexander Auldecambe, "An Unsentimental Report from Mexico," *Harper's Magazine* (March, 1966), 84.
[9] Florence Kluckhohn and Fred L. Strodtbeck, *Variation in Value Orientations* (New York: Harper, 1961).
[10] David C. McClelland, *The Achieving Society* (Princeton, N.J.: D. Van Nostrand, 1961), p. 434.
[11] *Ibid.*, p. 400.

The relevance of values of economic growth is shown in an international poll taken in eleven countries. Adults were asked what they thought was most important to teach children. In Japan 22 percent of respondents from lower socioeconomic status thought "ambition" was most important; in Denmark the figure was 9 percent, in Netherlands 3 percent.[12] In the post-war years the Japanese economic growth rate has often been the highest in the world.

Within the United States, where various sub-cultures have gathered, variations in achievement need and other values affecting school performance can be seen. Jewish educational values are described by Strodtbeck:

> . . . Jews have traditionally placed a very high value upon education and intellectual attainment. The Jewish parent was expected to provide as much education as the sons showed themselves capable of absorbing. . . . Learning in the "shtetl" society gave the individual prestige, respect, authority—and the chance for a better marriage. The Jews have a saying that "parents will bend the sky to educate their sons." The essential nature of education is further attested by the prestige associated with physical accomplishments. . . . Religious learning and the satisfactions of family life were not in this culture separated as they were in monastic systems.[13]

Jewish loyalty and obligations to the community, rather than just to the family, is seen by Strodtbeck as another important aspect of achievement because it liberated the individual from family constrictions.

Experimental Values

Experimental as opposed to traditional values should, in Dewey's view, serve the schools and the young as it served science and society. The child should no longer be a receptacle for old bits of information. He should be heard as well as seen, think and do as well as obey. Moreover the old authorities of revealed truth and texts should give way to the vitality of the inquiring mind. "Learning is active," he said, "it involves reaching out of the mind. . . . Literally, we must take our stand with the child and our departure from him. It is he and not the subject matter which determined both the quality and quantity of learning." [14]

Edward L. Thorndike, probably the most influential psychologist in the schools, advocated that the mind be trained by habit formations and strengthened stimulus-response bonds, a view that later found expression through the behavioral psychologist B. F. Skinner in programmed learning, using *fixed* subject matter and method. In contrast, Dewey wanted to, "abandon the notion of subject matter as something fixed and ready-made in itself, outside the child's experience. . . . The child and the curriculum are simply two limits which define a single process." [15] He directed the attention of some educators away from rote learning and outward in two directions: toward active learning, problem-solving and experimentation, the methods of science; and toward the individual child and his social learning. Schoolmen seemed more receptive to moving in the second direction than the first; the spirit of inquiry was, in the context of middle-class small-town America, less to be valued than sociability.

[12] Data provided by International Research Associates, from a release of March 13, 1958.

[13] Fred L. Strodtbeck, "Family Interaction, Values, and Achievement," in David C. McClelland, et al., Talent and Society (Princeton, N.J.: D. Van Nostrand, 1958), pp. 149–153.

[14] John Dewey, The Child and the Curriculum (Chicago: University of Chicago Press, 1902), p. 13.

[15] Ibid., p. 12.

Experimental inquiry never replaced the authority of text and teacher in the school. The teacher continued to ask the questions and students recited the answers. Even in science, the *method* of science—rigorous inquiry—took second place to its *substance* and to lecture-recitation of already discovered knowledge.

Nor was systematic inquiry applied to problem-solving in the schools, perhaps out of fear that, as Dewey put it, "If we once start thinking no one can guarantee what will be the outcome except that many objects, ends, and institutions will be surely doomed." [16] "Subjects" were kept in air tight compartments, and education was generally shut off from life, learning from doing, theory from practice and culture from vocation.

The most eloquent dispute in American education was over authoritarian versus democratic values in the school. The debate, interrupted by Sputnik, promises to resume if the assumed need for authoritatarian methods and "high standards" diminishes. Highly authoritarian attitudes among teachers and college professors have been reported and Herbert Stroup claims that in Germany, of all groups composing the Nazi party, teachers were the best represented.[17]

Feminine Values

The emancipation of women and their inclusion in the education system, one of the most significant school developments, has helped modernize this culture-bearing sex, but their presence in the schools has raised two unresolved problems.

1. Unlike European and Russian schools, the American primary and, to a lesser extent, the secondary school have been dominated by women who compose three-fourths of teaching staffs. Partly as a result the schools have acquired feminine values that reach even into higher education. These feminine and largely middle-class values have been antagonistic to the society's stridently masculine stress on courage, risk-taking, action, aggression, independence. Modern education, says Otto Fenichel, assumes that "aggressiveness is bad." Yet a person who is not capable of aggression, "is as much handicapped as a person who has lost his sexual abilities." [18]

2. Though girls are more academically successful in public school than boys, they are less likely to go to college or into advanced occupations; hence, considerable talent is lost to school and society.

Solutions to the problem might involve decreasing the school bias that favors girls, increasing opportunity for women in jobs and colleges, and altering the feminine mystique in order to raise female job aspirations.

Among the consequences of sex segregation in society and female domination in schools has been the neglect of science and technology. Other consequences have been emphasis on child development rather than subject matter, passive rather than active and aggressive virtues, and individual rather than group competition. The strength of these values in the school has made it easier for girls and for boys influenced by female domination to perform successfully in school and has tended to alienate the more masculine boys.

Gordon Allport, in isolating the following value factors—theoretic; economic; aesthetic; social; political; religious—found that women score higher

16 John Dewey, *Characters and Events*, p. xi.
17 Herbert Stroup, *Bureaucracy in Higher Education* (New York: The Free Press of Glencoe, 1966).
18 Otto Fenichel, *The Psychoanalytic Theory of Neurosis* (New York: W. W. Norton, 1945), pp. 584–589.

than men in aesthetic, religious, and social values, while men scored highest in theoretical, political, and economic values.[19] It appears to be the values more characteristic of women that prevail in the schools and those of men that dominate society.

Protestant Ethic

The Protestant ethic (individualistic, self-reliant, restrained, acquisitive) was a central feature of the value system that led to industrialization. This ethic permitted the Christian to read his own Bible in his own vernacular, conduct his own religious services, collect interest, and exploit others with a clear conscience. Early American schools were built on this ethic which, fortunately for education, asserted that Christians should read the scriptures and must become literate to do so. Time and the rise of other groups to power have softened the harsh excesses of this ethic but it remains a dominant value in schools and among "achievers" in the society.

Teamwork

Though many critics deplore the prominence, or even presence, of team competitive sports in schools, such sports may play a role in stimulating achievement and organization skills. Significantly perhaps, organized team sports are popular in developed, high-achieving societies and virtually absent in developing societies.

The team game may be both creator and creation of Western organization man, combining almost all elements of the achievement syndrome: activity, toughness, team work and competition, individual excellence, calculated risk-taking, sportsmanship, leadership, planning, speed of decision, perseverance, improvisation, organization skills, physical energy and agility, other-directedness, effort, and desire to win.

England, long a dominant world power, has been singularly devoted to team sports and has left, as one positive aspect of its colonial past, a sports interest in some developing areas. The general inactivity and passivity of children in many poor nations suggests that the introduction of team sports, along with good diets and health care, might aid national development. The declining emphasis on team sports in United States schools and society, along with heightened interest in the U.S.S.R. and Japan, may not be a wholly unmixed national blessing. While games may distract some youths from academic pursuits, they perform such a vital role in socializing the young and provide so much of what *esprit de corps* exists in the school, that they may not be as dispensable or commonly believed. Anomie, alienation, and underachievement seem most prevalent among youths who are least engaged in team games. Such sports provide a strong sense of belonging and group identity and thereby seem to counteract the alienation in modern society.

The Individual and the Group

Individualism has become virtually synonymous with the American way of life. Collective action has been esteemed in the immediate family and voluntary associations, but less in larger communities, or society generally.

American individualism differs from that of less "organization-directed" societies, such as the French or Arab, in that individual *achievement* rather than *eccentricity* is valued. While the American is forgiven many departures

19 Gordon W. Allport, *Study of Values* (New York: Houghton Mifflin, 1960).

values and ideology

from tradition that get results, the norms strongly discourage more superficial deviations in personal style of dress or conduct. He is a member of a team, usually a large organization, and he is expected to wear the team uniform.

"In contrast, the Arab manifests his individualism," says Hamody, "in his wish to assert differences, in lack of civic responsibilty, in an unruly spirit, and in the absence of cooperation with and trust in others." [20] Because of Islamic theocracy and the immutability of the Koran, "the bold, imaginative questioning of the nature of technological advances remained foreign to them," says Berger.[21] The mind was shackled but not the man, and individualism found outlets in personal style and behavior.

The superficial revolt of American youth in the early 'sixties, including the beat and the hip revolt of style, might have resulted from obstacles placed in the path of "imaginative questioning" by both school and society, as well as a growing distaste, for the team uniform and pressures for individual achievement. While attention to individual needs and growth has long been an ideal in American schools, overcrowding and school policy have permitted little individualism, independent study, or individual attention. Organization methods in the schools, in fact, tend to limit diversity, pluralism, and genuine individualism.

Nor has much successful small group work been permitted, despite general belief that peer interaction is essential to intellectual and personal development. In most societies the peer group is a primary source of information, security, authority. In some societies, such as the African Kikuyu tribe, loyalties and bonds among an age-group are stronger and more permanent than among family members. American schools have not used the principles of group dynamics to promote academic achievement though this might be especially useful among the disadvantaged where group ties are likely to be binding.

Out of loyalty and fear, it is common for prison inmates to endure punishment rather than betray others. Studies of work groups reveal a similar code. In the military, 61 percent of American soldiers in the Second World War said the one thing that kept them going was, "not wanting to let the other men down." Chinese strategy with United States prisoners in the Korean War was to separate individuals from their group and play one off against the other as a means of destroying social ties, identity, and ego. The prisoner was then offered a new identity. Ultimately, Schein writes, that which sustains humans is their personality integration born of secure group identity.[22]

Drug addiction has been successfully controlled through group therapy. "Synanon society," writes Lewis Yablonsky, "is able to involve and control the offender. This is accomplished through providing an interesting social setting comprised of associates who understand him and will not be outmaneuvered by his manipulative behavior." [23]

Weakening of family ties, urban anonie, and new knowledge about groups have stimulated some interest among schoolmen in groups, but heavier stress on individual competition in the schools, has more than balanced this interest. Students are encouraged to make friends in school clubs, but peer groups have not been used in the classroom for teaching or influencing values.

[20] Sania Hamody, *Temperament and Character of the Arabs* (New York: Twayne, 1960), p. 87.

[21] Morroe Berger, *The Arab World Today* (London: Weidenfeld and Nicholson, 1962), p. 31.

[22] Edgar H. Schein, *Coercive Persuasion* (New York: W. W. Norton & Co., 1961).

[23] Lewis Yablonsky, "The Anti-Criminal Society: Synanon," *Federal Probation*, 26:3 (September, 1962), pp. 50–57.

83

Human Relations and Scholarship

Usually the schools have preferred achievement measured by business values to achievement measured by scholastic values—although the two have been in constant tension in schools. Rejecting much traditional scholarship and often even intellectual development through inquiry and problem-solving, the school tended to move toward the social and psychic life of the child and "personality" development. The achievement "ideal" was often the "big man on campus," the all-around boy, athlete, class officer, popular, well-groomed, and headed for success in the business world.

Human relations came to be a more cherished value than scholarship. Human relations, as used here, is a generic term and it is not to be confused with human relations as a subject of inquiry into the sources and solutions of intergroup conflict. Only in 1961, following Sputnik and pressures to tighten school standards did the NEA Educational Policies Commission say: "The purpose which runs through and strengthens all other educational purposes—the common thread of education—is the development of the ability to think." [24]

In 1892 the NEA Committee on Secondary School Studies, in an early effort to define educational values, stated that the purpose of secondary education was to strengthen the various parts of the mind through discipline and training. Since secondary schools were then engaged chiefly in college preparation, representatives from higher education composed a majority of this committee, and President Charles William Eliot of Harvard was its chairman.

By 1918 the situation had so changed that a twenty-seven-man NEA Commission on the Reorganization of Secondary Education, containing only four college representatives, declared the purpose of secondary education was to, "develop in each individual the knowledge, interests, ideals, habits, and powers whereby he will find his place and use that place to shape both himself and society toward ever nobler ends . . ." [25] Seven cardinal educational goals were set: health, command of fundamental processes, worthy home membership, vocation, civic education, worthy use of leisure, and ethical character. The cardinal goals did not include scholarship, thinking, inquiry, training of the mind, intelligence, or knowledge. "No other committee or commission in this country's education history has had an effect comparable with that of the Commission on Reorganization," wrote Beck.[26]

Again, in 1938 the NEA Educational Policies Commission, based on a report of Charles W. Beard, declared the four objectives of education were: self-realization, social relationships, economic efficiency, civic responsibility." [27] As higher education grew in power relative to the secondary schools and international competition increased, schoolmen began to return to their 1892 emphasis on cognition and scholarship.

The schools have been repeatedly charged with anti-intellectualism by scholars and others. Professional education is still largely staffed, said Richard Hofstadter, particularly at the administrative levels by people who are far from enthusiastic about the new demand for academic excellence. Such adminis-

[24] "The Central Purpose of American Education," NEA *Educational Policies Commission*, 1961, p. 12.
[25] "Cardinal Principles of Secondary Education," NEA *Commission on Reorganization of Secondary Education*, 1918, p. 9.
[26] Robert H. Beck, A *Social History of Education* (Englewood Cliffs, N.J.: Prentice-Hall, 1964).
[27] "The Purposes of Education in American Democracy," NEA Educational Policies Commission, 1938.

84

trators, he says, have exalted the academically uninterested or ungifted child into culture heroes.[28]

According to Raymond E. Callahan, the "manifest anti-intellectualism" of school administrators was due to their close involvement with the business community. Many administrators, he said, prefer to be called "school executives" who spend their time managing personnel and attending to matters of finance and business rather than academic instruction.[29]

Teachers who seek out and are appointed to administrative positions, John Walton wrote, are most likely to be "teachers with the most generally desirable personal characteristics," such as "good appearance, the ability to get along with people, interest in community affairs, and conformity in dress, manners, and ideas." Central to their values, he said, and the values of people who occupy key positions in the community power structure are, "conservatism, provincialism, philistinism, and anti-intellectualism." [30] Fundamentally dependent upon business, salesmanship, and the art of making friends and influencing people, our culture has, says Mary Northway, "set extraordinary value on extrovert qualities." [31] Jerome Bruner adds that, "we have been a country in which doing has been taken as the mark of effectiveness in thinking." [32]

Human relations in the schools derived partly from genuine need: (1) The need to reconcile conflict in a pluralistic society. (2) The need to staff organizations with compatible people. (3) The growing realization that "success" came as more from knowing and influencing people, than from scholarship. (4) The growing anomie of urban life and the need for improved social relations.

Americans have believed that "making out" and "getting results" flow more from ability to work with people than from textbooks or classroom lectures. As one physicist put it: "We learn by gossiping with our associates." Human relations in the school gave rise to extensive extra-curricular "activities," voluntary associations in which to exchange information, pursue interests, and make friends.

Human relations values are also prevalent in colleges. In an Educational Testing Service study of freshmen at 23 colleges, 51 percent said their major interest in college was social life, extra-curricular activities, athletics, forming new friendships and carrying on "college traditions"; only 27 percent mentioned vocational goals and 19 percent the pursuit of ideas. At the end of the freshman year, students tended to take academic work even less seriously than on entry, to feel estranged from the faculty and eager for the company of other students; 40 percent said they were bored by classroom work "fairly often" or "always," and 60 percent felt there was no single faculty member to whom they were responsible or particularly close.[33]

Describing the values to which American education responded between the two World Wars, Conant lists: (1) free schools for all youth, (2) no differentiation in school organization which seemed to be antidemocratic, (3) heavy

[28] Richard Hofstadter, *Anti-Intellectualism in American Life* (New York: Alfred Knopf, 1963).

[29] Raymond E. Callahan, *Education and the Cult of Efficiency* (Chicago: University of Chicago Press, 1962), p. 1.

[30] John Walton, *Administration and Policy Making in Education* (Baltimore: The Johns Hopkins Press, 1959), pp. 60, 172.

[31] Mary L. Northway, "Outsiders: The Personality Patterns of Children Least Acceptable to Their Age Mates," *Sociometry* (February, 1944), 17.

[32] Jerome S. Bruner, *The Process of Education* (Cambridge: Harvard University Press, 1961), p. 73.

[33] *New York Times*, October 29, 1964.

emphasis on group activities which also interested adults as parents and spectators (team sports, music, marching bands), and (4) central focus on producing an upright, good citizen, tolerant, fair, committed to honest, representative government and "democracy as a way of life." [34] Conant tends to mistake the preferences of a few articulate spokesmen for the general practices of the schools, but insofar as these values were present they represent in part the influence of human relations.

Athletic and nonintellectual activities, in Conant's view, interfere with school work and should be minimized. His recommendations favor increasing and rearranging academic studies for the high school, with special attention to the "gifted" student, and his reforms for teacher training also deal mainly with academic requirements.[35]

On the other side, human relations criticisms of traditional scholarship are expressed in William Arrowsmith's claim that graduate education in humanities is "the creature of vested interests and dead tradition" and has "little pertinence to the real needs of men." The controllers of the humanities, he says, are "not humanists at all, but merely technicians of dead and living languages." [36]

The Soviets also complain of the deadweight and volume of academic learning. The student is taught so "much that he comes out of the higher school resembling a stuffed fish. One can have various attitudes toward the contents of the fish, but one thing is indisputable: It cannot swim. And then this fish comes to the research institute and demands more 'salinity' and wants to be garnished with sauce." [37]

Essentially the dispute has been between two groups—the academic establishment and the educational establishment—one emphasizing "subject matter" disciplines and the other "human relations" values.

Outside this contest have been at least three other tendencies.

(1) Civil rights groups who have emphasized egalitarian education more than changes in the educational content. (2) The "progressive" group, small but with articulate advocates such as social critic Paul Goodman who reject the values of both academic and educational establishments. Commenting on Conant's recommendations, Harold Taylor wrote, "the way to build a new curriculum for the development of the American teacher is to free him to move into those areas of knowledge where he can indulge himself in the love of learning." [38] (3) The "social reformers," composed of various elements, Theodore Brameld representing only one view:

> While repudiating nothing of the constructive achievements of progressivism, while recognizing also the importance both of essential knowledge and clear rational analysis, this philosophy commits itself, first of all, to the renascence of modern culture. It is infused with profound conviction that we are in the midst of a revolutionary period out of which should emerge nothing less than control of the industrial system, of public services, and of cultural and natural resources by and for the common people.

[34] James B. Conant, *Shaping Educational Policy* (New York: McGraw-Hill, 1964), p. 21.
[35] James B. Conant, *The American High School Today* (New York: New American Library, 1964).
[36] William Arrowsmith, "The Shame of Our Graduate Schools," *Harper's Magazine* (March, 1966), 51–52.
[37] "The Overstuffed Mind," *Izvestia*, December 28, 1960.
[38] Harold Taylor, "Future Implications and Repercussions of the Conant Report," *Freedom with Responsibility in Teacher Education*, 17th Yearbook of the American Association of Colleges for Teacher Education, 1964 Annual Meeting, Chicago.

values and ideology

Brameld advocates, "education which, through the schools of America and of all other democracies, could at last demonstrate its capacity to play no longer a minor but a major role in the rebuilding of civilization."[39]

Neither the academic nor the educational establishments have seemed notably interested in equal educational opportunity, free inquiry, or "rebuilding civilization."

Central Strains

Individual achievement and competition, as the core of the school's value system, have motivated effort among some students but simply created stress in others. The casualties of the system are often found among those who *cannot* or *will not* achieve according to school standards. Responses are resistance, resentment, ego damage, or an individual or organized opposition or rebellion. Many casualties also occur among the successful and among those who join the system. These may take the form of pressure-generated neurosis and insecurity. The system creates a rather large group of aliens, marginals, and outcasts, those who cannot "make out" in the system and those who reject individual achievement goals.

A central strain exists between individual achievement and equality, between expressed and practiced values. On record, the society believes in equality, but the practice is more often "every man for himself." This strain generates serious conflict between haves and have-nots. It also produces psychic conflict in youths who accept the incompatible values of the school, among scholarly students who are caught between their own drives to achieve and be "better than others" and their commitment to egalitarian ideals. The conflict would be particularly intense among youths from ethnic cultures that stress both individual achievement and social equality.

In early grades, schools teach unquestioned acceptance of the authority of adults and the society. In later years, particularly as students approach the difficult years of adolescence, some teachers may reverse this faith to one of scepticism and criticism. Internalized by the more intellectual students, these inconsistencies can produce serious value disorientation. Unless permitted to use their talents in movements to ameliorate the imperfections they learn to perceive, apathy and confusion may result. Similar problems are generated among disadvantaged youths who are drawn to individual achievement but find that inequalities (real or perceived) prevent it. Schools, perhaps contrary to their conscious design, actually prevent many students from achieving and being successfully competitive. The school performs, says Edgar Friedenberg, a Darwinian function. It, "endorses and supports the values and patterns of behavior of certain segments of the population, providing their members with the credentials and shibboleths needed for the next stages of their journey, while instilling in others a sense of inferiority and warning the rest of society against them as troublesome and untrustworthy."[40]

Though stressing individualism, the school's methods and organization tend to prevent the development of autonomous behavior, initiative, and independence. Since few alternatives to compulsory and standardized schools are available, "voluntarism," a central feature of American values, is virtually absent in the schools except in extracurricular activities.

[39] Theodore Brameld, *Education for the Emerging Age* (New York: Harper, 1950), p. 27.

[40] Edgar Z. Friedenberg, *Coming of Age in America* (New York: Random House, 1963), p. 49.

Stress on individual effort has obscured the value of "group" and "collective" effort in school and society. Preoccupation with individualism and development of the private sector of the society has tended to create disorder and indifference in the public sector. Moreover, it has tended to distract students from international interests to personal and private ones, even during a period of maximum American obligation to the world community. In few other nations is so little taught in schools about people of the world. In this sense, individual values and the lack of a strong social ethic or sense of public and collective obligations has led to serious parochialism in American education.

Social and egalitarian values may, indeed, be more important to economic development than individualist values. While the need for individual achievement in Japan, for example, is high, collective motives are also very important and may contribute significantly to national development. In the United States strong egalitarian *ideals* and pressures, and emphasis on team work have also contributed to development.

Some observers feel that individualism as a national ideology is not potent enough to create a great society. Perhaps the real threat, says sociologist Dan Dodson, "is that the ideologies on which our collective life rests seem to have lost their redemptive and regenerative abilities for so large a segment of American youth." [41] Elan is lacking, says Lerner, "the feeling of being on fire, a sense of mission, a sense that there are things worth dying for and worth living for. . . . I would say a people lives off its dreams." [42]

Schools often create anomie. While they offer a physical community for students, stress on individual performance tends to detach them from peers, creating isolation and anonymity. Conflict of school and home values also creates anomie, as does failure to prepare students for life. When schools fail to equip students to achieve in life what they aspire to, a great gulf between the desired and the obtainable is created. School achievement standards differ from those of society. Mastery of ancient history, for instance, is not likely to equip students for success in life. Often it is the "manipulator" rather than the "honest scholar" who finds a place in the sun.

Discontinuity may exist between the sheltered and ordered school community and the scepticism and permissiveness of the college "intellectual" community. Alienated college youth studied by psychologist Kenneth Keniston, were likely to do well in school, having been socialized by mothers to accept school authority and individual competition. While accepting these values pleased both school and mother, it also tended to separate students from peers, whom they needed to cushion the alienation and scepticism of authority generated by past-high school experiences. Entering the "life of the intellect" with faith in authority and desire to distinguish themselves, students may be shocked to find that the authorities he respects now tell him that "conformity" is a curse, that the society is decadent or without culture, and that those held up as role models are alienated and cynical.

Harold Rugg identifies value conflicts in school and society between: individualism and conformity, freedom and control, equality and inequality, materialism and idealism, agrarian and urban culture.[43] Jean Grambs points out

41 Dan W. Dodson, "Social Change as a New Frontier in Education," in *New Frontiers in Education* (New York: Grune & Stratton, 1966), p. 300.
42 Max Lerner, "The Individual and National Goals," in *Education: An Instrument of National Goals*, The Board of Trustees of the Leland Stanford Junior University, 1961, Cubberly Conference, School of Education, Stanford University.
43 Harold Rugg and William Withers, *Social Foundations of Education* (Englewood Cliffs, N.J.: Prentice-Hall, 1955).

values and ideology

conflict between conformity and creativity, competition and cooperation, the practical and the ideal, democracy and authority, puritanism and hedonism, chauvinism and internationalism.[44] More than in most societies, American values are eminently practical and adaptable. The high value placed on compromise and the adjudication of differences facilitates mediation between these opposing strains.

"Development" as a Quasi-Ideology

The sum of emerging American values might be termed a "development value system." It is not a traditional ideology in that it has no body of dogmas, guide to personal conduct, or blueprint for the future. Rather, it is flexible and adaptable and aims at broad targets—personal, social, economic, national, and international development. It transcends achievement values and goes beyond individual self-aggrandizement to advocacy of community responsibilities—to local, national, and international communities.

The term "development" recurs in discussions of the potential of physical and human resources—in phrases such as *developed* and *developing* nations, research and *development*, Agency for International *Development* (AID), community *development*, child *development*, *developmental* psychology.

What is to be done with the resources at hand? *Develop* them, of course. While idle physical resources have always been a challenge to national ingenuity, human resources and the resources of social organization have usually been conceived of as incidental, or at best instrumental, to the exploitation of physical resources. A shift has been occurring, however, from total concentration on economic, scientific, technological, and product development to concerns about human and social development. We have come to speak more often of educational development and to believe that education is the primary instrument of individual and national development.

"Development means economic, social, and political progress," said one influential public figure, "It means a reasonable standard of living. . . . Security is not traditional military activity—though it may encompass it. Without development, there can be no security." The central concept of security is, "a world of decency and development—where every man can feel that his personal horizon is rimmed with hope." [45]

[44] Jean Grambs, *School, Scholars and Society* (Englewood Cliffs, N.J.: Prentice-Hall, 1965).

[45] Robert S. McNamara, Secretary of Defense, speech in Montreal, *New York Times,* May 19, 1966.

youth culture
and the school
as a social system

eight

Youth is perhaps the only age group in Western societies that has a unique culture, one that distinguishes it from other age groups. The badges of this subculture—styles of dress and behavior—are proudly displayed as evidence of growing maturity. The subculture is based in a mixture of increased *autonomy* derived from new economic power and ability to escape adult controls, and *dependency* derived from prolonging adolescence into ages when youth were formerly employed and independent.

Youth has been less influential in the United States than in nations where they are more likely to be employed or politically involved. Marginal to both political and economic systems, but with abundant leisure and purchasing power, American youth has asserted itself as a cultural entity, distinctive from other groups in style, appearance, and behavior. "The prominence of this youth culture in the American secondary school," says Parsons, "is, in comparison with other societies, one of the hallmarks of the American educational system; it is much less prominent in most European systems." [1]

---

[1] Talcott Parsons, "The School Class as a Social System: Some of Its Functions in American Society," *Harvard Educational Review* (Fall, 1959), 29:4, 315.

College

Subcultural Variations

Youth from different backgrounds and high school cliques tend to choose different kinds of colleges. Many of these colleges, in turn, stamp their students with their own cultural mark. For this reason, getting into the "right" college and staying there has been a major source of anxiety for many middle-class youth and their families.

Four college subcultures are identified by Clark and Trow: the *Collegiate* culture whose chief value is to have fun and socialize; the *Vocational* group, interested in jobs and a diploma; the *Academic*, which identifies with the serious concerns of the faculty and whose main interest is said to be "knowledge"; the *Nonconformists*, who are often hostile to college administration, concerned about "ideas" and "search for identity," and who set themselves apart by a very distinctive style of dress and behavior.[2] College subcultures appear to be of declining relevance.

College students, according to Kenneth Keniston, are increasingly motivated by vocational interests, particularly the lower-income students.[3] They now prefer the professions to business, largely out of a desire for socially useful, prestigious, and profitable work. Those opposed to exclusive vocationalism, Keniston says, fall into three groups: the "activists," well-liked and above average students, who have a commitment, not to a political belief or ideology, but to a moral position on specific issues; the "disaffiliates" or the alienated who have resentfully withdrawn from American society and who resist entering adult life; the "under-achievers" who reject themselves rather than society. "All are non-ideological or anti-ideological. All oppose or despair about large-scale political and social planning," he says. None want to reform society.

In a study of a small number of Harvard students in the mid-'50s, Keniston concluded that significant numbers of middle-class students are "alienated" from the society. These students, he found, were products of tight-binding, seductive and possessive mothers on one hand and of technological values that fragment both society and the individual on the other.

The "alienated" avoided athletic competition or group activity. They tended to be humanities majors with aesthetic interests that led to rejection of American culture as crass and materialistic. They also tended to be honors students, nonjoiners, and nonparticipants. Confronted with a problem, they "took off" and withdrew. Many were fascinated by drugs, especially hallucinogens, sought new experience, and lived almost completely in the present. They were aggressive only in argument where they tended to be dominant, active, negative.

Technological values of the society, according to Keniston, impose too great a burden of change on youth, shattering community life and integrity of personality. These values, he feels, are concerned with efficiency and productivity rather than human needs and result in a serious deficit of tradition, order, ideology, and planning in the society.

[2] Burton R. Clark and Martin Trow, "Determinants of College Student Subculture," in R. T. N. Newcomb and E. K. Wilson, eds., *The Study of College Peer Groups* (Chicago: Aldine Publishers, 1960).

[3] Kenneth Keniston, "Faces in the Lecture Room," *Yale Alumni Magazine* (April, 1966), 20–34.

Secondary School

Cliques appear in many schools as early as the seventh grade, and adolescents are notoriously prone to tight clique formation. Such cliquishness, innocent when not exclusive, is actually encouraged by school policy and extra-curricular activities, and by the school's failure to promote activities in which heterogeneous groups of youth participate. Cliques and sub-cultures vary greatly among schools and make generalizations difficult. Clique snobbery, however, seems as prevalent among "intellectual" students as among the "social" crowd.

High schools are studied more than other schools because of the national absorption with "teen-agers" and because youth culture is most obvious there. Also in the secondary school American youth from various strata confront each other for the first, and often the last, time. In elementary schools, students come from homogeneous neighborhoods. In college, students come mainly from the middle class, and later, on the job and in residential neighborhoods, the same class separation occurs.

Most studies of high schools show that, at least in large schools, social cliques stratify students and dominate school life. Usually these cliques are based on social differences, but they are not, as Talcott Parsons points out, a simple mirror of adult stratification. The composition and influence of these cliques are affected by many factors, including geographic area, conditions of the time, ethnic and class composition of the student body, and the size of schools. Usually, however, there is an elite and an outcast clique, with various groups in between.

Harold Phelps and John E. Horrocks, studying a small Ohio community, concluded "the degree of emancipation from adult control appears to be a most important influence in the formation of patterns of informal adolescent group activities and attitudes." [4] In the 'twenties the Lynds observed in Middletown that the high school, with its athletics, clubs, sororities, fraternities, dances, parties, and other extra-curricular activities, was a fairly complete social cosmos.[5]

In 1941–42 Hollingshead looked at the small midwestern community Elmtown and found three groups of students: (1) An elite of leaders in extra-curricular activities and social affairs. (2) The "good kids" comprising about two-thirds of the students and including various sub-groups such as "the Lutheran gang," "the Catholic bunch," the "farm kids." (3) The "grubby gang," "set off from the other students for many reasons—unfortunate family connections, personality traits, lack of cooperation with teachers, living in the wrong part of town." [6]

The Hollingshead and Lynd studies, classics of their time, may not be very relevant to contemporary schools. Youths under twenty now spend $10 billion annually. Earning power has made it possible for youth to escape parental and school control and has changed their behavior and culture. Middle- and working-class youth are now likely to drive cars or motor cycles that put distance between themselves and adults, and they are more likely to spend time at the drive-in movie or hamburger stand than at the school-centered drugstore. The drive-in, the nearby lake, the drag strip are places where conduct not permissible nor even possible, at the local drugstore, is sanctioned by peers.

[4] Harold R. Phelps and John E. Horrocks, "Factors Influencing Informal Groups of Adolescents," *Child Development* (March, 1958), 24, 84.
[5] Robert and Helen Lynd, *Middleton, op. cit.*
[6] August B. Hollingshead, *Elmtown's Youth* (New York: Science Editions, Inc., 1961)

youth culture and the school as a social system

The defensive wall separating youth from adults is made more impenetrable as youthful conduct becomes more at variance with the articulated value system of the home and school and as parents are less able to guide the choices and careers of their children. Thus, while the Lynds found that the youth of Middletown imitated their elders, William Riggle more recently saw the youth who ran the school as being unusually mature and independent of adult control.[7]

White, Black, and Gray

In one large suburban California high school, Riggle found four distinct groups: the White Shoes (about 10 percent of students); the Gray Shoes also known as the Nobodies (a middle group comprising about two-thirds of the students); the Black Shoes or Hards who wear dark clothing (about 25 percent of students); and last, a group of Outcasts (about 3 percent of students).

The White Shoes, resembling their hero Pat Boone, and the Black Shoes, resembling Elvis Presley, had many things in common though occupying opposite poles of the schools social scale. Both groups were unusually mature and independent of adult control; both had a well-defined subculture of their own; both lived fast and hard lives and were much involved with peer groups, parties and strong living. While the White Shoes appeared well-mannered and respectable, the Black Shoes were bent on being the unrespectable, yet one girl observed: "A White Shoe is nothing but a Hard with manners." [8]

Doing well in school was not prized by White Shoes, but "there is a constant contest going on as to the one with the most clothes, or the most expensive kind; and there is also the struggle as to who dates the most or has the best-looking boy friend." White Shoes consider a "good or proper home background" of utmost importance. They enjoy physical activity, and are competitive, aggressive, ambitious, proud, self-confident, and optimistic. They value a sparkling personality far above mere academic or classroom proficiency. Soap and water seem to be their single most distinguishing trademark. The boys express utter contempt for the Hards, whom they say are dirty, grubby, and greasy. The girls wear little make-up, and they like the "clean-cut" look, while boys take only those shop courses where they won't get dirty.

School activities are centered on extra-curricular groups—called "co-curricular" by the school to emphasize their importance. The girls like dancing, but baton twirling and cheerleading are "out." Journalism is "in" for the girls because it allows them to follow the boys' sports activities. Student government is very much "in." "Some White Shoes undoubtedly will become leaders on Main Street . . . for the values and attitudes they learned early to espouse in school are certainly the ones that seem to be the most esteemed on Main Street." [9] One teacher said, "They are narrow-minded, set in their opinions, and quite conservative in outlook." [10]

As for the Black Shoes, many come from trailers and "cracker-box" houses, broken homes and families that can't afford fashionable clothes. Although most are Anglos, many are Mexicans, Italians, Negroes. "Those students often receive poor grades because they resent authority and a school that is run by 'snobs.' " [11]

[7] William H. Riggle, *The White, The Black, and the Gray: A Study of Student Subcultures in a Suburban California High School* (University of California, Berkeley, unpublished doctoral dissertation, 1965).
[8] *Op. cit.*, p. 15.
[9] *Op. cit.*, p. 79.
[10] *Op. cit.*, p. 70.
[11] *Op. cit.*, p. 83.

youth culture and the school as a social system

"Their uneasiness, insecurity, and inability to cope successfully with the educational establishment no doubt accounts for much of their rebelliousness against it." [12] As one girl said: "Hards act like no one can hurt them but deep inside they are really hurt many times. Hards are made fun of, and they try to act real tough to make up for it." [13] One Black Shoe girl said: "This school makes us feel we don't belong here." [14] Unlike the White Shoes they are strongly egalitarian and reject the notion that some people are better than others. It is an "absolutely disgusting mess," said one Gray Shoe girl about school cliques, when students are "treated like rats and fleas from the gutter, when from behind their backs they are laughed at and made fun of because their dresses are old and mended." [15]

Youth Values

A national survey in the early 'forties reported that 72 percent of teenagers gave as a major concern in school "how to get along with people," while only 14 percent listed academic achievement. Other major concerns, most of them related to "being liked," were: gaining or losing weight; getting stage fright in front of a group; wanting new friends and more dates; wanting to be more popular; wanting to improve posture and developed self-confidence.[16]

Based on interviews with 100 students, Friedenberg concluded that high school students prefer the "regular" boy or girl—perhaps even the mediocre to the off-beat.[17] "To most students," Friedenberg says, "a taste for intellectual activity for its own sake is exotic and suspect." They resent others who, "do what they feel like doing," or who can function effectively in solitude without caring much about group support.[18] These observations predated the newer emphasis on academic rigor in the schools and the burgeoning of the teenage "Beatle" culture which, even in suburbia, encouraged novelties of dress, views, and behavior.

James S. Coleman reports about several midwestern high schools that: "Athletics is far and away more important as a value among high school students than intellectual achievement. . . . And the school itself seems to encourage rather than to discourage this." [19] Though Coleman favors reducing the dominance of athletics, he notes that athletics "has a democratizing effect, breaking up organization based on background and reconstituting it on the basis of common activity and achievement." [20] Athletics serves an important function in motivating students, he says, and makes it possible for all students to identify with the school and to have collective goals. The democratizing mechanism of sports, he concludes, is particularly important for boys, who are, "less involved in school than girls and get poorer grades. If it were not for interscholastic athletics or something like it, the rebellion against school, the rate of dropout, and the delinquency of boys might be far worse than they presently are." [21]

12 *Op. cit.*, p. 136.
13 *Op. cit.*, p. 136.
14 *Op. cit.*, p. 167.
15 *Op. cit.*, p. 188.
16 H. H. Remmers and D. H. Radler, *The American Teenager* (Indianapolis: Bobbs Merrill, 1957).
17 Edgar Z. Friedenberg, *Coming of Age in America, Growth and Acquiescence* (New York: Random House, 1963).
18 *Ibid.*, pp. 65–66.
19 James S. Coleman, *Social Climates in High Schools* (Washington, D.C.: Government Printing Office, 1961), p. 33.
20 *Ibid.*, p. 33.
21 *Ibid.*, p. 39.

94

Though a rather pervasive alienation and dissatisfaction among youth is reported by Kenneth Keniston, Paul Goodman, and others, a national sampling of youth indicated that American teenagers were typically purposeful, pragmatic, and quite satisfied. The 17 year olds reported that the world is fast, competitive, and modern—more competitive at 17 than at 13 and also more impersonal.[22] Eight percent of the total group and 22 percent of Negroes said they were less happy at 17 than they had been at age 8 or 9. Many complained that nobody listens to them, at home or at school. Sex was reported the major topic of discussion in high school and the car the most valued possession. About a third said that what they like most about themselves is their friendliness.

Teens must function in two worlds, that of youth culture and that of their home and ethnic culture. The declining importance of Italian-American youth gangs, says Francis Ianni, derives from the elimination of their causes. "Culturally, the sudden break from a strong, family-centered adolescence made strong peer-centered associations inevitable." [23] Also important was, "a sense of cultural inferiority to which the teenagers responded by banding together."

One of the significant features of the older teen in the Jewish community is a strong college orientation; 65 percent of Jewish teenagers attend college. Although their attitudes are like their non-Jewish peers, says Boroff, they "tend to live in a vast, self-enclosed Jewish cosmos with relatively little contact with the non-Jewish world. . . . Marriage, particularly for girls, is a prime value" . . . and the cultural consumers—book buyers, theater goers, etc.—are largely girls. Among Jewish youth, the "more ambitiously intellectual find themselves at odds with a culture which they regard as repugnantly materialistic." [24]

According to Himes, two modes of aggression tend to distinguish Negro teenagers: [25] personal aggression exhibited by low-prestige youths, and the aggression of social protest which has been led by college youth. Negroes, in a sense the "newest ethnic minority," have already moved out of the stage of defensive gang formation. They have moved into the cities, into channels of upward mobility, group protest and action. Perhaps the most effective high school social action involving matters of educational policy has been carried on by Negro teenagers. Though college youths have formed many social and political action groups, however durable they may be, American high school students rarely have, though such activity would be likely to have a profound effect on school policy.

Dropout and Delinquency

A three-year study of high school dropouts by Robert Vinter concluded that dropout is mainly the fault of the school system not of the students who quit school, and that, "All of the pupils studied were capable of completing high school and began their careers motivated to do so." [26]

Between 40 and 50 percent of youth drop or are pushed out of high school before graduation, and most apprehended delinquents come from this group. School cliques and stratification contribute to their fate. "Esther and her friends," Robert Havighurst writes, "are caught in a vicious circle. Since they are not accepted in the social life of the adolescent peer culture, they make

[22] "The Teenagers," Newsweek (March 21, 1966).
[23] Francis A. J. Ianni, "The Italo-American Teen-ager," The Annals (November, 1961), 338, 78.
[24] David Boroff, The Annals, op. cit., 79.
[25] Himes, The Annals, op. cit., 91.
[26] Unpublished study reported in New York Times (November 23, 1966).

a life for themselves with other adolescents who are not accepted. This gives them a bad reputation, and they have more difficulty than ever in their relations with their schoolmates. School becomes a prison. . . ."[27]

The junctures at which adolescents need to be "handled," Kingsley Davis notes, tend to come earlier and be more troublesome for dropouts than for the college-bound.[28] In China and Japan, he says, parental control continues after adolescence, but in the United States there is an absence of definitely recognized and consistent patterns of authority and a major goal of American adolescence is emancipation from the family. Adolescence is a period of crisis in which profound changes are imposed by rapid physical growth and change, heightened sexuality, pressure to leave home, necessity to make decisions about the future, the need for jobs and financial independence, and a sudden awareness of the realities of life.

Schools add to the burden by failing to prepare students for adolescence and for the "realities" of later life. The student drops out or leaves school, says Davis, "with a hoard of abstract knowledge, but with little knowledge of the concrete situations he must negotiate in order to get along. The harder he studies the more unfit he becomes for ordinary day-to-day existence. Above all, there is such a long interval between learning and application that the incentive to learn often flags and must be bolstered by an amazing system of planned competition and artificial rewards."[29]

Dropouts and others may suffer "culture shock" on entering the labor market—". . . the revulsion the young worker feels against the routine of repetitive work, the fatigue of hard work, the commands of an authoritarian supervisor, dishonest business procedures, the deviant personal habits of fellow workers, and the insecurity of work."[30]

Identifiable subcultures, such as Riggle's Black Shoes, may be formed by the dropout. William F. White's, observations of "street corner society" in an Italian slum distinguish between "college boys" and "corner boys," the dropouts who form a close peer group which gives status and security but also impedes upward mobility.[31]

The Normal and the Deviant

"Because of tensions inherent in the modern position of youth," says David Matza, "they have been vulnerable to a variety of deviant patterns. These deviant patterns manifest a spirit of rebelliousness and have taken three major forms in American life: delinquency, radicalism, and Bohemianism."[32]

During the early 'sixties a cultual exchange with England reached the average American teenager. The result was an exurberance of gay eccentricity which brought the early teens for the first time into a culture-making role. The English style was, in turn, influenced by working-class culture. Motifs from this source were first seen in the work of the "angry young men," novelists and playwrights,

[27] Robert J. Havighurst and Hilda Taba, Adolescent Character and Personality (John Wiley and Sons, 1949), p. 39.
[28] Kingsley Davis, "The Sociology of Parent-Youth Conflict," in "The Psychology of Adolescence," Annals (November, 1944), 236, 8–16.
[29] Davis, op. cit.
[30] Delbert C. Miller and William H. Form, Industrial Sociology: An Introduction to the Sociology of Work Relations (New York: Harper, 1951), p. 574.
[31] William F. White, Street Corner Society (Chicago: University of Chicago Press, 1937).
[32] David Matza, "Subterranean Traditions of Youth," Annals (November, 1961), 338.

whose "plain" heroes were working class and whose work had social and political rather than psychological overtones.[33]

Dwight MacDonald has called teen rock and roll dancing a "Dionysian revolt against a predominantly Apollonian society," expressing spontaneity and ecstasy as opposed to self control.[34] It may also be an expression of working-class spontaneity and vigor, and of the "animal spirits" of the early teens. The elevation of working-class anti-heroes (such as the Beatles)—neither handsome, "classy," or cultured, but just "plain kids"—has been a leveling and democratizing aspect of teen culture.

While rebellion elsewhere often took the form of political radicalism, in the United States it was expressed more often in withdrawal or negativism. In Britain, where youth is more politically involved than in the United States, John Mays points out that the angry young men were "social reformers rather than world rejectors," and their movement was an "intellectual and artistic resurgence as much as a desire to throw the whole of our society over-board." [35] In Britain it is the "angries" rather than the "rebels without a cause" who "epitomize the more serious youth's reaction to the mess and injustice which he has inherited from his elders."

Mays feels "it is the task of education in the widest sense of the term to promote and regulate social change, and to do this successfully means, among other things, assisting young people to rebel against certain unworthy aspects of the social structure." [36] Friedenberg demands attention be focused on moral issues raised by youth, and deplores the "overriding commitment of our culture to working compromises." [37] Adults live in a world where ideals are simply distant goals, and where altruistic motives are cherished in public and selfish ones acted upon in private. Youth lives in a pre-life world and their virtues are "courage and loyalty; while the necessity for even a moderate degree of compromise humiliates them greatly." [38]

Partisan statements in behalf of youth, such as Goodman's *Growing Up Absurd*, while registering a clear and plaintive protest against adult handling of youth, often neglect plausible alternatives for adults who are already whirling with confusion about adolescents. What seems evident is that youth needs a lofty but practical statement of societal goals—heroic, adventurous, and challenging, and they need a role in formulating and achieving these goals. Together with adults, they need to reshape the world of work, so that meaningful and rewarding jobs may be open to them.

Youth is far from centers of power and change in the society, and the institutions that guide and are closest to them—family, school, church—tend to be the most traditional. ". . . with one major exception," says Parsons, "the social structures bearing most directly on youth are likely to be rather far down the line in the propagation of the effects of change. These are the family and the school, and they are anchored in the local residential community. The major exception is the college, and still more, the university, which is one of the major

---

[33] In most places, young-teen culture is working class, and older-youth culture is more influenced by collegiate and middle-class groups.

[34] Dwight MacDonald, "Profile—A Caste, a Culture, a Market, II," *New Yorker* (November 29, 1958), 34.

[35] John Barron Mays, "Teen-Age Culture in Contemporary Britain and Europe," *Annals* (November, 1961), 25.

[36] Mays, *op. cit.*, p. 32.

[37] Friedenberg, *op. cit.*, p. 10.

[38] Friedenberg, *The Vanishing Adolescent* (New York: Dell Publishing Company, 1959), p. 30.

loci of innovation and which can involve its students in the process more directly." ". . . schools, especially elementary and secondary schools, are on the whole probably more conservative in most respects than are the organizations that employ the fathers of the children." [39]

Youth have not begun to participate in the national society. Their ideals are lofty but their perimeters confining. School and society limit them to the service of self and their immediate milieu; and seldom offer the opportunity for society-serving activity.

Elementary School Classroom Interaction

Research on the elementary school classroom as a social organization has been summarized by John C. Glidewell.[40]

DEVELOPMENT AND STABILITY. Within several weeks after entering the classroom, children acquire a social position based on three assessments: emotional acceptance, or how much the child is liked by others; perceived competence, or the assessment of ability and achievement in school work; social power, or influence over others. The child with social power may not be the most popular but he will usually be liked by other children of influence. These social positions remain quite stable over several years. Most children know what their position is but some, whom teachers may inaccurately judge to be emotionally disturbed, are not aware of status. Newcomers to a class are likely to be more competent but less well-liked than students already in the class.

CENTRALITY AND DISPERSION. A typical American elementary school classroom appears to be composed of interlocking subgroups of students. It has been suggested that these are usually arranged in a hierarchical order but this has not been proven. Sometimes the attributes of emotional acceptance, competence, and social power are concentrated in a few individuals in a classroom and sometimes they are widely dispersed. Social power, or influence over others, is more related to acceptance by others than it is to academic performance.

THE TEACHER. Teachers who are more accepting and democratic tend to affect the social relations of children but not their academic performance. They tend to reduce anxiety of students, stimulate more pupil interaction and autonomous work by students and to disperse social power and perceived competence among students. Teachers have more effect on the classroom when they seek to influence the dominant rather than the submissive students, though the submissive ones are more easily influenced by teachers.

SOCIAL ANTECEDENTS AND CONSEQUENCES. Social class and racial differences affect but do not determine the social position of children. The influence of these factors grows as the children get older. To be accepted a child must, however, come from the dominant social class in the community, at least as a marginal member. Not all teachers come from the middle class and those who do, appear to set different standards for children from non-middle class backgrounds.

[39] Talcott Parsons, "Youth in the Context of American Society," *Social Structure and Personality* (New York: The Free Press of Glencoe, 1964), p. 171.
[40] John C. Glidewell, *et al.*, "A Report of a Work Group to the Committee on Social Structure and Socialization of the Social Science Research Council," The St. Louis County Health Dept., 801 S. Brentwood Blvd., Clayton, Mo., April 15, 1965.

youth culture and the school as a social system

PERSONALITY ANTECEDENTS AND CONSEQUENCES. Acceptance by other children does not appear to be based on physical fitness or intelligence. "Significant relationships exist among self-esteem, position in the classroom social structure, achievement, and mental health. Development of social skills usually requires conformity to adult and peer norms." [41]

GROUP DYNAMICS. According to Neal Gross, the main contribution of sociologists studying the classroom has been sociometrics, the study of social relations within the class. The attitudes and behavior of the individual appear to be "strongly linked to those groups to which he belongs or aspires." These reference groups constitute 'anchoring points' which have to be considered in inducing changed behavior. [42]

Sociometry indicates, says Norman Gronlund, that between 11 and 22 percent of pupils in various grades are neglected or ignored by classmates. [43] Group dynamics has explored group influence on individuals and methods of changing behavior. Some principles produced by the investigations are summarized by Dorwin Cartwright:

> If the group is to be used effectively as a medium of change, those people who are to be changed and those who are to exert influence for change must have a strong sense of belonging to the same group.
> The more attractive the group is to its members the greater is the influence that the group can exert.
> In attempts to change attitudes, values, or behavior, the more relevant they are to the basis of attraction to the group, the greater will be the influence that the group can exert upon them. [That is, for example, a union has more influence over worker behavior on the job than in the voting booth.]
> The greater the prestige of a group member in the eyes of other members, the greater the influence he can exert.
> Efforts to change individuals or subparts of a group which, if successful, would have the result of making them deviate from the norms of the group will encounter strong resistance. [Thus, children cannot be persuaded to achieve in school if such achievement will violate the code of their group.]
> Strong pressure for changes in the group can be established by creating a shared perception by members of the need for change, thus making the source of pressure for change lie within the group. [People inside a group are more effective in bringing about change than people outside it.]
> Information relating to the need for change, plans for change, and consequence of change must be shared by all relevant people in the group. [Communication among members of a group are needed to bring about change. Overt hostility is often communicated in such exchanges and sometimes gets out of hand.]
> Changes in one part of a group produce strain in other related parts which can be reduced only by eliminating the change or by bringing about readjustments in the related parts. [Changing the behavior of nurses, for example, will create strains in their relations with medical groups above and below them, and these relations must be considered in bringing about change.] [44]

While some teachers are aware of "interpersonal relations" in the classroom and some of the techniques of group dynamics—"role playing," buzz

[41] Glidewell, op. cit., p. 90.
[42] Neal Gross, "Some Contributions of Sociology to the Field of Education," *Harvard Educational Review* (Fall, 1959), 29, 4.
[43] Norman E. Gronlund, *Sociometry in the Classroom* (New York: Harper, 1959).
[44] Dorwin Cartwright, "Achieving Change in People: Some Applications of Group Dynamics Theory," *Human Relations* (1951), 4:4, 381–392.

groups, process observers, post-meeting reaction sheets, and feedback of group observations—this knowledge is rarely used for motivation or therapy.

Though educators and researchers have been concerned about democratic attitudes, "the evidence available fails to demonstrate that either authoritarian or democratic leadership is consistently associated with higher productivity. In most situations, however, democratic leadership is associated with higher morale." [45] Sarane Boocock reviews the sociology of learning, a relatively unexplored field, and identifies four influences (classroom, school, peer group, outside-school) on student learning. Her two general impressions are that the quality of research is uneven and that little can be said with certainty about how social factors affect students.

> The classroom, the core of the school learning system, presents the most confusing picture. We cannot yet say just what it is that the effective teacher is or does. . . . Satisfying group relations, often perceived as the panacea for all education problems, are not related to learning in any direct or consistent way. From what is now known, there is no one type of teacher, teaching, or classroom organization which produces the "best" results with all students in all areas of academic endeavor.

As for the whole school and its community:

> . . . until certain gross inequalities in schools—which put some socio-economic status, racial and other groups at a disadvantage before they ever enter the formal school system—are balanced, large numbers of students will never achieve any real interest or success in learning.
>
> Finally, research on student peer groups, which contains some of the best designed and most conclusive studies, makes it quite clear that many young people will not apply their best efforts to learning tasks unless this is consistent with the norms of their informal cliques and friendship groups. The need here is for some imaginative applied research, which will point to ways of channeling these potentially powerful peer group influences to promote intellectual goals.[46]

[45] Richard C. Anderson, "Learning in Discussions: A Resumé of the Authoritarian-Democratic Studies," *Harvard Educational Review* (1959), 29:201–215.

[46] Sarane S. Boocock, "Toward a Sociology of Learning: A Selective Review of Existing Research," *Sociology of Education* (Winter, 1966), 39:1.

city
and community
nine

The school is physically located in the community and its most intimate attachments to the society are or should be there. Indeed, one community, the city, and its schools have become symbols of both the distress and the future prospects of the society. The community is a source of support, indifference, or opposition to the schools, but in any event, it is where the action is, where the children live, and where the school is located.

Seventy percent of Americans now live in urban areas; 75 years ago two out of three people lived in the country. Seventy percent of the population is now squeezed onto one percent of the total land area. There are at least a million more people living in city slums than on all farms, and at least a million more will move from farm to city in the near future.

Although a majority of the population moved from rural to urban areas during this century, political, educational, and other institutions have kept many of the old roots in the farm and small town. Rural areas, moreover, have controlled most state legislatures and been overrepresented in Congress. Over half the members of the Senate and nearly half the members of the House of Representatives have rural backgrounds. In most states, city and suburban voters generally have been only one-fifth to one-half as well represented in state legislatures as small towns and farm areas, though the balance may shift following reapportionment.

101

Problems of the Cities

The power of "states' rights" at the national level, the rural control of state government, and the political dependence of cities and their schools on state funds and control, have deterred the cities from solving their own problems and reducing some of the shocking pathologies of the "inner city." New York City, for example, received in 1961–62 $197.00 in state aid for each student while the average in the rest of the state was $314.00.

Although the society and schools have become increasingly urbanized, the structure of school administration, the method of teacher training, the methods of financing were all designed to service schools of a bucolic society, where there were relatively uncrowded and untroubled cities. Moreover, the middle class that dominates city schools has been interested in preparing their own children for the school race but much less concerned about other children.

City distress has been intensified by the exodus of the middle class to suburbia and the entrance of disadvantaged populations into the central city. In the new suburban areas the middle class set up school systems that began to rival and attract resources from the city schools. Conant has pointed up the ability of the suburb to pay for good schools, and the resulting disparity between education in slum and suburb.

Until the Second World War cities enjoyed a pre-eminent position in attracting the best teachers then graduating from colleges. But since then, suburban systems, offering higher salaries, newer buildings, smaller class size, better equipment, parking facilities, safer neighborhoods, and more tractable students have forced city schools to consider less-qualified candidates.[1]

In addition to the power squeeze of rural areas, the competition of suburban systems, and the entrance of large numbers of impoverished minorities, city schools suffered from two other major internal problems: (1) In the cities, as compared with smaller communities, citizens and parents have been greatly underrepresented on school boards in relation to the bureaucracy. In the typical small town or suburb, a school board of nine citizens can cope with a system of four or five schools and a dozen or so bureaucrats, but in the city they cannot hope to manage a system containing hundreds of schools and thousands of bureaucrats. In addition, the average citizen is remote from all centers of power —physically and psychologically. He has no representatives from his neighborhood or even district on the school board. He typically does not even know the name of school board members, or when or where the board meets, nor is he likely to know where the bureaucracy's headquarters are located, or how a citizen can petition for redress of grievances. He has then almost no acess to the centers of power, except to teachers at the neighborhood school. (2) Perhaps as a consequence of the foregoing, the powerless and growing minorities in the cities have been grossly underrepresented in the bureaucratic structure itself. Daniel Griffiths reports that of 777 top officials in the New York City system, including board members, superintendents, and principals, only six were Negroes in 1963, or 0.8 percent of the total.[2] Four years later almost no change was perceptible.

[1] Robert I. Sperber, "Modern Trends in Recruiting, Selecting and Assigning Teachers for the Cities," *Urban Education* (Buffalo: University of Buffalo Foundation, Winter, 1965), I:2.

[2] Daniel Griffiths, *et al.*, "Teacher Mobility in New York City, 1963"; an unpublished report. See Patricia C. Sexton, "City Schools," *Annals*, American Academy of Political and Social Science, Vol. 352 (March, 1964), 95–106, for an analysis of ethnic and class representation and conflicts in city schools.

102

City public schools have also, in a sense, been threatened by the rapid growth of the Catholic parochial school system. Parochial schools have relieved somewhat the financial distress of public schools, but they have often turned citizen attention away from the public schools and attracted groups that might otherwise have helped to integrate public schools. The relationship of city public and parochial schools has not been carefully studied.

The urban crisis is partly a consequence of the neglect of social planning, and the failure to organize general citizen participation, particularly among the disadvantaged. The city is unplanned. It grew as best served the interest of industrialism and was built for profit, not wholesome living. The schools are part of that planless growth. The most serious disorder caused by this lack of planning is the presence of the ghetto school and community in the inner city.

Countermeasures might include: (1) a national plan to encourage population movements to desired areas in the country, create new and integrated cities, disperse industry and jobs to reduce loads on the city, provide incentives for the dispersal of cities to the countryside; (2) a city plan for metropolitan areas which would integrate populations by bringing middle-class groups back into the city and form heterogeneous planned communities (as with improved urban and human renewal), reconstruct the city and its pattern of life through experiments such as the federal Demonstration City program to rehabilitate slum life, and aid the integration of new immigrants of disadvantaged populations into the city.

Methods used to decrease segregation in city schools have included the bussing of students into integrated schools, the redistricting of schools, the creation of educational parks, and metropolitan area planning. None of these has decreased de facto segregation in the city, however the growth of Negro and the decline of white populations have in fact increased segregation.

Those who live in city ghettos expose themselves and their children to a peculiarly urban pathology, anomie, and to growing populations of childless individuals—and they must send their children to chronically disabled schools. New York City operated schools where in 1965 about 29 percent of teachers were "regular substitutes" not fully licensed to teach (probably a better record than most large cities). Between 1960 and 1965 there was a turnover large enough to staff the entire 51,000-teacher system. One of every four schools in the city was more than 50 years old and considered ready for razing, and 250 of the city's schools were operating over capacity. Such disabilities are not equally shared among schools within a system but have been borne most heavily in the past, and to a significant extent even in the present, by low-income groups, as my study of one city school system indicated.[3] The city lacks power to govern itself, to make laws, and to tax itself. Financial problems are chronic and growing more acute. The cost of operating a municipality tends to mount geometrically rather than arithmetically as the city grows, and the tensions within the city tend to mount in the same way.[4] Other perplexing problems of cities have been:

[3] Sexton, Education and Income, op. cit.

[4] The financial bind in New York City, for example, is chronic. The city's 1965 budget was for $4 billion. Almost 60 percent of this was composed of items that could not legally or safely be lowered (water, fire, etc.), including hospitals and city medical care (12.7 percent), welfare (13 percent) (four of five recipients were unemployable, mothers, children, the elderly). The other 40 percent were made up of items that should be raised—schools (21 percent), police (7.6 percent), local poverty programs (1.9 percent)—leaving 2 percent for recreation and 7.6 percent for everything else. Federal and state aid were 28.5 percent of the city's income. Real estate taxes brought in 36.4 percent of funds, sales tax 10 percent, and business tax 5 percent. The city had a debt service of $1 billion, acquired

103

1. Use of cities for solely commercial rather than human purposes.
2. Poverty as a function of low wages, inadequate supply of jobs, lack of incentives in public welfare policy, and employers' desire for a large pool of low-wage workers.
3. Gross inequities in the distribution of wealth.
4. Lack of aggressive public initiative in solving community problems.
5. Gross inefficiency of public bureaucracies.
6. Anomie, inadequate communication among citizens, inadequate neighborhood spirit and community organization.

In one of the earliest urban studies, Robert Park concluded that the city was more than a place but was also a state of mind, a new way of life, and a body of traditions. The major interest of the "Chicago school" was in social disorganization and the ecological process: the contraction and dispersion of people, centralization and decentralization of functions, segregation, invasion, and succession.[5]

Community Concepts
Some educators have insisted on a partnership between school and neighborhood. The community, in this view, should be brought into the school—into its curriculum, staff, and policy-making—and the school should reach into the community via adult education and involvement in community life. Children should be taught to use and develop community resources, and the community helped to solve its problems.

A movement to "recapture community life flourished in the 1920's" said Julian Woodward, and as a result of the influence of the progressive education movement, the early 'forties saw an "unusual stress laid by the schools on localism, on community-centered instruction and participation in community life, on the community as the seat of the democratic process." [6]

The "community school" has, of course, been more often a reality in suburban and rural areas than in city slums. After some neglect, the community school concept was revived during the 'sixties out of new interest in slum neighborhoods. Anti-poverty programs employed youth in neighborhood conservation programs, engaged in community action, set up new education programs, and tried to stimulate interaction between school and community. Federal initiatives aimed at urban rehabilitation and the development of both physical and human resources. Other stimulants to community interest have been: the application of *community development* techniques here and abroad and the use of local self-help programs to solve community designated problems; Peace Corps efforts in schools and communities; volunteer, and other programs in the slums.

In most communities, but particularly in the urban slum, the school is the dominant institution, the major representative of the outside world, the largest employer, and the prime "opportunity" resource. Yet school and community are usually aliens. The school opens at 8:00 and closes at 3:00. Teachers

---

mainly during the depression. A large proportion of both city and school expenditures go to payment of interest on debts. The city maintains a bureaucracy of 291,000 civil servants. Local government spending has gone from $9 billion in 1946 to $50 billion today and may double again by the '70's. Cities spend half their money on education.

[5] Robert E. Park, *et al.*, *The City* (Chicago: University of Chicago Press, 1952).

[6] Julian L. Woodward, "Is the Community Emphasis Overdone?" *Harvard Educational Review* (October, 1941), 11:472–480.

city and community

and administrators live elsewhere and often have as little contact as possible with the neighborhood. Many schoolmen blame family and community for student failures but insist that what is outside school walls is not their problem. Interaction might break down communication barriers, provide a voice to the community, aid student performance, and reduce reference group confusion among childen who now live in two separated worlds.

Various personnel changes might also improve the present situation in which a foreign element—middle-class school staff—enters the school each morning and withdraws each afternoon. Such changes might include the employment of local people as school aides in both instructional and new instruction roles; the use of local people and teachers as community organizers; the placing of local people on elected school boards, advisory committees, or appeal boards; and the provision of special housing to enable teachers to reside in school neighborhoods.

Spanish Harlem

Spanish Harlem, An Anatomy of Poverty was my own effort to understand, by living in the community several years, the organizational structure of an urban "slum." [7]

The book represented an effort to find out what "life" is like in an urban "slum." What "indigenous" organizations, formal or informal, exist in the community? What institutions exist there—school, church, government, social agency, business—who runs them and how do they "help" the community? Who has the power to make important decisions? What is the record of self-help and protest?

Particular attention was given to community organization, community development, social-action techniques, the effects of urban renewal on the community, and the transition of institutions as they served different ethnic migrants, including Puerto Rican and Negro.

Among my findings were that the largest and potentially most influential organization was the Roman Catholic Church, yet it played a minimal role in community affairs and social action. In a community composed almost exclusively of Puerto Ricans, Negroes, and remnants of the older Italian group, the most influential people were likely to be white, Anglo-Saxon Protestants, and almost all the official organizations, agencies, and institutions were headed by whites. Public schools were almost totally segregated (unlike the parochial schools) and headed by whites. Since the publication of that volume, the Catholic Church has become an active leader in the community and has helped mobilize citizens around public school power issues.

The University and the Community

In higher education, the upsurge of interest in community has resulted in new degree programs and courses on city schools and communities; a new dialogue between schoolmen, scholars, and the community; and a proliferation of new community research.[8]

[7] *Spanish Harlem* (New York: Harper & Row, 1965). In *The Urban Villagers*, Gans described a Boston Italian community which, though slated for urban renewal, was able to maintain a village atmosphere and considerable neighborhood feeling. Herbert Gans, *The Urban Villagers* (New York: The Free Press of Glencoe). Clark's *Dark Ghetto* discusses the Negro power structure, the psychology and pathology of the ghetto, the school as a nucleus ghetto institution, and strategies for change. Kenneth B. Clark, *Dark Ghetto, Dilemmas of Social Power* (New York: Harper & Row, 1965).

[8] A useful section on conducting community school studies is found in Lloyd and Elaine Cook, *A Sociological Approach to Education* (New York: McGraw-Hill, 1960).

105

The most promising innovation is the new symbiotic relation developing between some urban universities and the cities and the neighborhoods which surround them. In the past, these relations have been marked by conflict and invasion. Slums surrounding some urban universities have "invaded" university grounds and the universities have countered by buying property in the slum for university use. In the future, depending on the availability of funds and incentives, the relationship may become cooperative. The university may then "extend" its knowledge and resources into the community, as in agricultural extension (discussed in the final chapter), to aid in solving community problems. The university's role may then become one of positive participation in urban life. As it is, the city university is typically remote and isolated from the growing distress that surrounds it.

Community Definition

In discussions of "community" it is usually pointed out that various kinds of community exist. There is a community with a geographic boundary and there are, as Roland Warren notes, new concepts of community as "people," community as "shared institutions and values," community as "interaction," community as "distribution of power," community as a "social system." [9]

A promising direction in community studies, says Warren, is the attempt to apply social-system analysis to communities and to study structured interaction between two or more units, aimed at goal attainment, the integration of member units, and the tension or conflict between them. He further notes that the great change in community living is the decline of community cohesion and autonomy and the increasing orientation of local communities to "extracommunity systems of which they are a part"—the state or national society.[10] Urbanization has changed and obscured the older community concept, erasing geographic boundaries, neighborhood ties, and substituting, if anything at all, communities based on occupational, religious, and ethnic ties.

The most relevant community for the school is the old geographic community, the neighborhood school. In inner-city areas populated by people without families, it is the absence of the school and the children that produces the "stranger" and the "lonely crowd." People in a neighborhood meet each other and share things in common through their children (in New York, their dogs). In the city slum the potential of this "sharing" has not been realized because people are transient and unorganized, nor has the potential of sharing in communities that transcend the immediate neighborhood been realized, which is also due to the failure of communication and organization.

The "community school" aims to stimulate sharing and interaction. The newer community concept can be distinguished from the old and moribund "local school" concept, on which the American system is presumably based, in the following ways:

The Local School

In the city, quasi-centralized authority.
Little citizen representation in central authority.
Absence of nontraditional forms of citizen participation.

[9] Roland L. Warren, *The Community in America* (Chicago: Rand McNally and Company, 1963).
[10] Warren, *op. cit.*, pp. 53–54.

Belief that the local geographic or neighborhood community is the only one relevant to the schools.

No involvement of schools in solution of community problems.

The Community School

Small organizational units.

High level of citizen involvement in decision-making at every level.

Participation of citizens from the community on staffs, in paid school and community jobs.

Involvement of school, students, parents, and citizens in solution of pressing community problems (health, housing, adult education, and so on).

Active involvement of the school in all forms of traditional and non-traditional adult education.

Use of community organizers—both teachers and community people—to aid school-community liaison and to stimulate various forms of community organization.

Participation in joint efforts with other agencies and organizations in the community.

Realization that the local community is dependent on many other communities especially at national levels, and the organization of the total community to petition for assistance to the schools at all these levels.

It must be kept in mind, of course, that this "community school" concept is a relatively new one and that it should be subject to the same rigorous evaluation as other innovations to determine its contribution to the stated *goals* of school and community.

research
and development
strategies:
the future
of the American
school

ten

Schools have lagged behind more modern organizations in their capacity to change, and have generally lacked the incentives, resources, and knowledge needed for change. Research and development (R&D), generator of both agrarian and military-industrial revolutions, may also stimulate a revolution in education and the social sciences. Even in the natural sciences, R&D is so new that an estimated half of scientific research has been done since 1950, and about 70 percent of all scientists who have lived are still alive. R&D operations are now so vast in noneducational areas that, in the ten-year period ending in 1963, about $100 billion had been spent in the United States by both public and private sources on research in all areas.

Expenditures by the federal government on R&D have risen at an astonishing rate. At the beginning of the Second World War, the annual federal investment in R&D was only $74 million, about half of it in agricultural research. By 1965 it had risen to $15.2 billion, almost 90 percent of this being spent on defense, atomic energy, and space exploration.

Just about 1 percent of the gross national product is being invested in research. In some industries, such as chemical plants, R&D spending runs as high as 20 percent of total budgets. *Less than one-tenth of 1 percent* of the total education budget is spent on educational R&D. The chief *single* source of funds has been Cooperative Research of the United States Office of Education, although some four to six times as much is spent by all other sources—

local, state and private—combined.[1] Educational R&D has had a low priority and budget. In 1956 Cooperative Research had a budget of $1 million, a figure which rose to $5 million by 1962. R&D spending in the United States Office of Education in 1958 was about 1 *percent* of that allocated to R&D in the Public Health Service and was *less* than that spent in such agencies as the Forest Service, Commercial Fisheries, or the Bureau of Sport Fisheries and Wild Life.

Private foundations have invested rather heavily in education, and most universities have made intensive efforts to stimulate research among their faculties. In higher education, $27 million was spent on organized research in 1940, $373 million in 1954. In 1965 higher education got 15 percent of its annual revenues from federal R&D funds, or a total of $1.8 billion; some universities received as high as 40 percent of their operating budgets from this source. More than two-thirds of federal funds went to only 25 of the 2,000 institutions of higher learning, most of the major recipients being on the East and West Coasts. Government now provides about one-quarter of the income of private institutions of higher learning, mostly in research grants.

Federal research programs, says Seymour Harris, "fundamentally change the nature of the university." [2] While its traditional function has been the dissemination of existing knowledge, its new function is the creation of knowledge through R&D.

Traditions of Research

The traditional approach to research has been to *do* it, *process* the data, *write it up* in a professional journal, where it resides until used as a reference in someone else's research. The volume of educational research "stored" in this manner almost defies summary. The task is aided by several key publications issued by the American Educational Research Association, a department of the NEA and the chief "collector" and "storer" of research findings.

The weightiest of these publications is the *Encyclopedia of Educational Research*—1564 pages. A similar volume, *Handbook of Research on Teaching*, 1218 pages, presents reviews of research for use by the classroom teacher. Three NEA periodicals—one for teachers, *What Research Says to the Teacher*, and two for researchers, the *American Educational Research Journal*, and the *Review of Educational Research*—make available new research that has been "written up."

The *Encyclopedia*, because it indexes its more than 100 subject titles only in alphabetical order, presents an unfocussed picture of educational research. These discrete titles, when categorized, seem to deal almost exclusively with the teaching-learning process and inner-school matters. Only a few titles index subjects that are outside the school proper. Although ten pages of review are devoted to the subject "Personality," the national economy and its influence on education cover only about four pages. This emphasis reflects the traditional belief that only what happens within a classroom or an individual affects learning.

The *Encyclopedia* also reflects the influence of human relations and educators' values in the schools. Of the alphabetic list of some 190 subjects, only 33 pertain to the *subject matter* of learning. One of the three R's, "writing," is missing among the title subjects. "Agricultural education" is included but not

[1] Lindley V. Stiles, "The Cooperative Research Program," in Benson, *Fisheries and Wild-Life, op. cit.*, p. 293.

[2] S. Harris, *et al., op. cit., Challenge*, pp. 3–4.

"urban" or "suburban" education. Only seven titles cover academic subjects: classical languages, English, mathematics, arithmetic, modern languages, science, social studies. The sciences—including all the physical and life sciences—are treated as one. Similarly, "social studies"—including history, civics, economics, and geography—are treated as only one topic, though vocational topics such as "business education," "commercial arts," and "industrial arts" are all given separate treatment.

The *Encyclopedia's* major concerns appear to be (1) administration and organization; (2) the child and aspects of his development and guidance; (3) school staff; and (4) research methods.

In titles relating to the child, "development" is frequently listed—including mental, motor, physical, social, emotional development, and "developmental psychology." Psychological topics are given much attention, including "behavior problems," "mental health," "psychological services," "aptitudes," and so on.

The only *issue* of controversy listed is "academic freedom." Though "gifted childern" and "physically handicapped children" are among the titles, the "disadvantaged" or their equivalent are not. Nor are "civil rights" or related topics included. "Cultural differences" and "intercultural education" are listed but they do not cover civil rights material, nor do "desegregation," "Negro education," and similar topics appear. Though much research on "stratification" exists, no discussion of the subject is included. Nor are authority, status, inequalities, opportunity, politics, social action, or power dealt with. Only eight items treat of topics *outside* the schools: "community," "family," "church, state and school," "foundations," "federal relationship to education," "national economics and education," "parent-teacher relations," "population change."

A related document, *Research Relating to Children*, issued by the United States Children's Bureau, describes studies in progress on growth and development (30 pages); personality and adjustment (46 pages); educational process (28 pages); exceptional children (33 pages); the child in the family (17 pages).[3] Social, economic and cultural influences cover only eight pages; in these only five studies were reported on public policy issues, economics, or social issues— about one-and-a-half pages of the total report.

The *Handbook* discusses educational research theory and methods of teaching various subjects. The major topics covered are: teaching methods, teacher personality and characteristics, instruments and media of instruction, social interaction in the classroom, the social background of teaching (mainly factors that influence people to enter teaching). The *Handbook* summaries seldom present clear guides to the practitioner. On the subject of methods, for example, it reports: ". . . different teaching methods emphasize different principles and neglect others. Since this is the case, there is little likelihood that any one is superior to any other when the over-all effects of teaching are apprised."[4]

On "teacher's personality and characteristics," it reports: "Despite the critical importance of the problem and a half-century of prodigious research effort, very little is known for certain about the nature and measurement of teacher personality, or about the relation between teacher personality and teaching effectiveness. The regretable fact is that many of the studies so far have not produced significant results."[5] On the "use" of education research, the depressing report is: ". . . even sound research products have not generally met with

---

[3] *Research Relating to Children*, Bulletin No. 18, HEW, Welfare Administration, 1965, U.S. Govt. Documents, U.S. Govt. Printing Office.

[4] *Handbook*, p. 500.

[5] *Ibid.*, p. 574.

research and development strategies: the future of the American school

enthusiastic adoption and wide-scale implementation. However, even this may be partly related to the deficiencies of much research. The practitioner may sometimes be smarter than we think." [6]

As for "social background of teaching," the *Handbook* observes that research has been mainly limited to responses to the question: How do social and cultural forces "affect the probability that capable people will enter or remain in teaching?" [7] Wages, working conditions, and power relations are not mentioned.

The periodical *What Research Says to the Teacher* covers much the same subject matter as the *Handbook*. Of its 30 issues up to 1965, eleven were directly concerned with learning and subject matter. Others dealt with "personality adjustment of individual children," "understanding interpersonal relations," "mental health," "physical fitness," "creativity," "listening," and such matters.

The *Education Index* is a cumulative author and subject index to some 166 educational periodicals. The *Index*, first published in 1929, is issued each year. A useful semi-monthly publication, *Education Summary*, reports concisely on research and development in education.[8] The academic journal *Sociology of Education* is the sociologist's main contribution to educational research and thought.[9]

Impact

This voluminous research has come to few conclusions and had almost no effect on the schools. Schools, of course, are relatively impervious to change. Although the time lag in medicine between research and adoption is estimated at two years, in the schools it is estimated at between 30 and 50 years. The lag results not only from resistance in the schools but from the clear inadequacies of educational R&D, its narrowness, fragmentation, and myopic concern for the classroom at the expense of factors in the school *system* that affect the classroom. A further problem has been inability to disseminate and diffuse research findings to their potential users, or to influence policy decisions.

Educational R&D, like schools themselves, has generally been under the control of school administrators and other traditional elements of school and society. R&D efforts of local schools, state departments of education, the N.E.A., and even to a large extent the United States Office of Education have usually been under the direct supervision of school administrators.

"By and large, with obvious exceptions," says Martin Mayer, "educators in positions of power and visibility are not among the most able members of their profession. Organizations like AASA and ASCD, and the Educational Policies Commission of the N.E.A., have an almost unbroken record of fearful objection to the introduction of ideas not yet vetted by the shopkeeper communities which control school board elections." [10]

Daniel Griffiths suggests that "the major impetus for change in organizations is from the outside" rather than from administrators, that the degree and duration of change is directly proportional to the intensity of stimulus from

---

[6] *Ibid.*, p. 670.

[7] *Ibid.*, pp. 802–803.

[8] *Education Summary*, Croft Educational Services, 100 Garfield Ave., New London, Connecticut.

[9] *Sociology of Education*, edited by Leila Sussmann, published by the American Sociological Association.

[10] Martin Mayer, *Innovation in Education*, Matthew B. Miles, ed., *op. cit.*, p. 625.

111

the outside, that "the number of innovations is inversely proportional to the tenure of the chief administrator," and that the "more hierarchical the structure of an organization, the less the possibility of change." [11]

When a business organization flounders, new management is usually brought in. The new head may bring in many of his own men and completely reshuffle executive offices. Such new management may be needed in the schools, from the top to the lowest levels. Yet administrators, who now control R&D, cannot be expected to objectively examine their own roles or initiate change that would threaten their own positions. Although school administrators tend to favor research aimed at problem-solving (unlike many scholars who work with them in R&D efforts), their definition of "problems" usually excludes investigations that might disturb the management *status quo*.

"School superintendents, principals and teachers," said Nicholas Murray Butler, former president of Columbia University, "are to the last degree impatient of criticism and suggestions. . . . The better among them excuse the worse, and the worse grow abusive. This attitude is sustained by the agents of the more unscrupulous among the schoolbook publishing houses, who are selling hundreds of thousands of worthless old text-books each year . . . They are satisfied with the schools as they are."

Upgrading schools may require *outside* control of R&D efforts and an external monitor to evaluate school and management performance. Perhaps educational reform might require the abolition, or major alteration, of schools as we know them now. If so, the schools can hardly be expected to perform their own autopsy, or even major surgery. At best the schools may apply first aid to their injuries; they can hardly go much further.

Theory and Goals

The most critical and neglected part of educational R&D seems to be hypothesis and theory-formation rather than methodology. "Theory development," says Robert Travers, has not been the "forte of those whose interests are directed towards life's practical problems." It has "hardly been an identifiable activity within the field of education, though there have been some attempts to reshape theories drawn from the outside." [12] Theory from the outside, however, is often as irrelevant to the main thrust of American education as it is to the problems of society. In one study, for example, 30 outstanding American sociologists reported a belief that theory had little relation to empirical research, and that the important problems in sociology were not being dealt with by theory, research, or their own work. The problems most often mentioned as major ones in contemporary sociology were "social change" and "social problems of economic development." [13]

A large obstacle to successful R&D is the lack of clarity about educational goals. School systems are so vast that they move awkwardly at best toward the definition and achievement of goals. Often they are distracted into detours and dead-ends. Or they may assume that requiring teachers to write their "goals" on the board each day provides adequate direction for the system.

[11] Daniel E. Griffiths, "Administrative Theory and Change in Organizations," *Innovation in Education*, M. Miles, ed., *op. cit.*, pp. 429–436.
[12] Robert M. W. Travers, "A Study of the Relationship of Psychological Research to Educational Practice," in Robert Glaser, ed., *Training Research and Education, op. cit.*, p. 538 (Pittsburgh: University of Pittsburgh Press, 1962).
[13] Mihailo Popovich, "What the American Sociologists Think About Their Science and Its Problems," *The American Sociologist*, ASA (May, 1966), 1:3.

research and development strategies: the future of the American school

Schools exist to do "something" to the student, but what? Students, teachers, administrators, parents, colleges, and society all have different and often conflicting goals. Obviously, it is impossible to decide *how* to achieve goals or how to measure their achievement until the goals themselves are properly clarified. Confusion has existed in educational R&D over three kinds of goals: those relating to personnel, academic achievement, and primary purposes.

Personnel Goals

Many R&D efforts have been diverted to personnel production as an end in itself, one unrelated to the purposes such personnel will serve. R&D conducted by higher education, for example, has often been distracted to targets related to their own traditional functions, that is, the recruitment and training of teachers, administrators, and researchers. These are often treated as ends rather than means to the primary goal of educating students. Because of this diversion, a good deal of training is irrelevant to the primary goal. Schools of education, for example, rarely question whether what they "do" to teachers has any significant effect on what is "done" to students. Usually they judge teacher performance by their own arbitrary standards rather than by the effect teachers have on students. Similarly, it is usually accepted as "given" that the training of social workers and guidance people and the extension of their "services" into the school have a positive effect on students. One six-year study of 400 potentially delinquent girls, however, showed that even total intervention by social workers, including case work and group work, had no effect on the achievement or behavior of the girls in or out of school.[14]

Academic Goals

A goal of some R&D which is closer to the primary target has been directed toward student academic achievement. The clearer definition of this goal has resulted largely from the concerns of higher education and the effects of such concerns on parents and other groups. Starting in the nineteenth century with Hebart, Mann, Parker, and Rice, attempts have been made, unsuccessfully, to introduce scientific method into the schools by showing the relation between school practices and students' academic achievement. Many current R&D projects are continuing that effort, but without notable success.

Primary Goals

In general, schools, parents, students, and others have accepted academic achievement goals. Such acceptance derives from the authority of higher education, the value placed on achievement, the desire to raise literacy levels and "qualify" students for college and good jobs. Also important is the fact that no other clear "standard" or goal has been set. Paper-and-pencil tests of academic achievement are a far easier and more tangible proof of student growth than any other measurements available.

Academic standards of achievement are open to question on two counts. (1) Does academic achievement represent the exclusive or even primary goal of education? (2) If indeed it does, can even the best tests of academic achievement measure either genuine intellectual excellence, or ability to use academic learning in real-life settings? Indeed, does conformity to arbitrary "academic standards" actually limit intelligence and creativity and eliminate the most unique, inquiring, and productive minds?

[14] Henry J. Meyer, Edgar F. Borgatta, and Wyatt C. Jones, *Girls at Vocational High,* An Experiment in Social Work Intervention (New York: Russell Sage Foundation, 1965).

Tests seem inadequate even for measuring academic achievement, a relatively simple variable. Complex behavior such as autonomy and creativity may not be measurable at all. Stress on academic achievement in schools may, therefore, be largely attributable to the relative ease of measuring it. Almost 130 million "standardized" tests are given in schools each year, or almost three tests for every student in the first grade through college. Test costs run so high that in New York City, for example, one dollar is spent on tests for every five dollars spent on books. Most of these tests measure academic achievement.

The question of school standards involves the related matters of *qualifications*—the standards applied for admission to jobs and higher education—and *certification*—the awarding of tangible proof (certificates and diplomas) that standards have been met and that the candidate is "qualified."

All of these pertain to goals and practices which, considering their significance, should be subject to public review. Such investigations would require inquiries into whether the training given students and teachers actually produces qualified performers; whether tests and standards now in use measure more than narrow pencil-and-paper achievement; and whether selection procedures based on these standards pick the most able performers. E. M. Forster puts the issues more colorfully. "The pseudo-scholar often does well in examinations (real scholars are not much good), and even when he fails he appreciates their innate majesty. They are gateways to employment, they have power to ban and bless. . . . As long as learning is connected with earning, as long as certain jobs can only be reached through exams, so long must we take the examination system seriously. If another ladder to employment was contrived, much so-called education would disappear, and no one be a penny the stupider." [15] In fact, preliminary findings of investigations by sociologist Ivar Berg and others indicate that those of less education do better than those of high education in many occupations, the less educated having lower absenteeism, turnover, and job dissatisfaction.

Methodology

When experimental programs are being conducted by the schools or others and are not under the control of the researcher-evaluator, the numerous methodological problems that result include: clearly identifying the often vague goals of these experiments, getting access to data in the schools, finding suitable measurements especially for nonacademic variables, controlling experimental variables, developing research methods suitable to action programs that continually change directions. Evaluation under these circumstances is rather like trying to measure the height of a child who is not only in motion but running off in all directions. Only when the researcher is in complete charge of the experimental program can many of these problems be eliminated.

The lack of a systematic and centralized approach to educational R&D in the past has resulted in heavy losses and needless duplication of research data. Data have been collected for many thousands of fragmented studies, at great cost of money and effort, analyzed for certain limited purposes, reviewed for academic journals, and then lost. There has been no accumulation of raw or coded data. Each researcher must repeat what his colleagues have laboriously done before him—go out into the field, give achievement and other tests, punch student scores on data cards, and after some statistical analysis, put the cards

15 E. M. Forster, *Aspects of the Novel* (New York: Harcourt, Brace, 1927), pp. 24–25.

in his closet until they are thrown out. An estimated 10 percent of all research collects data that already exist but cannot be located. In the past, the principal storage place of published research findings has been the *Encyclopedia of Educational Research,* mentioned earlier. The field of chemistry, which produces about 30 finished research studies for every one in education, has an automated storage and retrieval system. The Defense Memory System simplifies research by making available some 3000 Congressional defense-related items in the form of conventional printed abstract, microfilm, data processing cards, and computer tapes. To provide similar education data retrieval, the United States Office of Education has created twelve Educational Research Information Centers (ERIC), providing a national network, with headquarters in Washington, D.C., to acquire, abstract, index, store, retrieve, and disseminate the unpublished educational data which is accumulating at a phenomenal rate.[16] Beyond that, large "banks" of data from national surveys are available on computer cards and tapes at some R&D centers and the United States Office of Education.

No educational equivalent of the National Institutes of Health has existed —a national center where problems are carefully defined and examined. A cancer research center exists, but there is not, for instance, a comparable reading research center. Nor has there been an equivalent of military R&D operations (the Army's Human Resources Research Office—HumRRO—and Special Operations Research Office—SORO, or the Air Force's use of the Rand Corporation, or the Navy's Center for Naval Analysis). To provide more systematic R&D and dissemination of the information, federally sponsored R&D centers and Regional Laboratories have been established, but these are still too much in their infancy to be evaluated.

Policy Change

Until general citizens' demands for better schools produced changes in public policy and new federal initiatives, researchers tried, usually unsuccessfully, to disseminate and diffuse their findings to the schools. These attempts usually took the form of efforts to change attitudes and practices of school staff through conferences and in-service training. Some spoke of creating "change agents" and producing packages or systems of materials for easy adoption.

Many ignored, when they did not actively oppose, the use of research to influence *public policy* and the intervention of such policy into school practices. Public policy initiatives which have occurred have taken the following forms:

1. Specific grants to schools for designated programs rather than traditional general grants which schools may spend as they wish.
2. The withholding of funds from schools that do not comply with federal policy, as in desegregation.
3. Grants to R&D in specific high-priority fields, such as science, to begin and complete the cycle of school adoption. At M.I.T., a National Science Foundation grant produced in two years, starting in 1956, a curriculum, texts, laboratory guides and equipment, teacher's guides, films, and college-entrance tests. In 1959–60 these products were given to manufacturers for commercial

[16] Educational Research Information Center, Division of Research Training and Dissemination, Bureau of Research, U.S. Office of Education, 400 Maryland Avenue, S.W. Washington, D.C.

exploitation. The N.S.F. then financed teacher training institutes in the use of the new methods. In a short time a radical change was achieved in the school's science curriculum.

4. Extension of the Program Planning Budgeting System to provide school accountability for expenditures and performance. PPBS is a budgetary system that bases funding on specific objectives and a review of performance. It calls for clear definition of education goals, definition of budget categories in terms of programs that pursue these goals; identification of program costs; measurement of the effectiveness of programs in terms of progress toward goals; determination of the most economic means to achieve these goals; regular review and revision of goals, programs, and budgets in the light of experience and of changing conditions; and long-range planning and cost projections.

Experimental Variables
and Strategies of Change

Innovators have sought formulas for improving schools and have found a wealth of possibilities from which to choose. As a result, hypotheses and remedies for school ailments have proliferated. National surveys of traditional practices suggest that, of hundreds of variables tested, only a few are related to such school outcomes as achievement, college entry, school retention. Project Talent reported, tentatively, that only teacher salaries, teacher experience, the number of books in the school library, and per pupil expenditure were, in the secondary school, related to such school outcomes.[17]

Though "change" has become a password, most of the numerous changes being adopted are superficial. A catalog of change in one state, for instance, announced that in the 15 post-Sputnik months, public schools more than doubled their rate of instructional change. Most of the changes consisted of selecting new textbooks. "Despite the number of new programs introduced, schools as *structured institutions* have remained stable. Few innovations have embodied changes in the kind of people employed, in the way they are organized to work together, in the types of instructional materials used, or in the time and places at which teaching occurs." [18] The highest rates of change were in science, math, and foreign languages. The higher the grade level (and the closer to college entrance), the higher the rate of change. In grades four to six, changes were initiated only about 60 percent as often as in high school, and in the primary grades only about 40 percent as often. Ability levels served by change were: below-average ability, 280 new programs; average, 359; above average, 785. A total of 53 new programs served the "handicapped."

New technology and material may offer promise of significant change, but unless carefully evaluated, they may swamp the school with expensive products, a new space-science idiom, and irresistible knowledge about how to "sell" customers. Those who will produce and sell educational innovations, including those who build schools, the technology producers, and text publishers, need encouragement to enter the educational marketplace but they also need careful public monitoring. Often it is the educational "panacea" and strategy with the hardest push from educators or sellers, rather than the closest relation to goal achievement, that receives most attention from schoolmen.

The list of experimental variables that might be used in R&D to improve

[17] Project Talent, *op. cit.*
[18] *1961 Catalog of Educational Change*, Commissioner of Education, State Education Department, Albany, New York, p. 27.

research and development strategies: the future of the American school

traditional education can only be suggested here, as they have been to some extent in preceding chapters; they include the following:

EMOTIONAL AND PHYSICAL FACTORS. The child is a physical and emotional as well as intellectual being, yet the effects on student performance of good nutrition, health and medical care, adequate rest, recreation, and a wholesome emotional life have never been tested. Chemicals have been used with remarkable results in treating mental disturbance but their effects on learning have not been gauged, nor has the effect of group or individual therapy.

LANGUAGE. Simplifying, phoneticizing, and otherwise changing the written English language to correspond more with the spoken, might greatly ease the student's central academic task of mastering this rather difficult and irregular language.

SCHOOLS. An almost infinite number of changes might be made in schools. Among those considered are: (1) changes in the division of power among administrators, teachers, students, parents, citizens, government groups, and minority groups; (2) changes in standards of rating, qualifying, and certifying used in selecting students and school staff; (3) changes in school organization methods, as previously discussed, providing competition among schools and greater consumer choice for students and parents; (4) simple increases in, and equalization of, school expenditures; (5) fresh approaches to staff: for the teaching staff, improved rewards and incentives for teachers, redefinition of the teacher's role and greater specialization to make job performance and training easier, the use of nonprofessionals in new roles, and improved on-the-job training of teachers; for the administrative staff, the use of new standards for selecting administrators so that nonschoolmen might be chosen and freedom for superintendents to choose their own staffs; (6) changes in school stratification and segregation practices; (7) improved methods of traditional instruction (including better lectures and discussions, use of the discovery method, and more independent study and field work) and improved materials of traditional instruction (including better texts and workbooks, better libraries, and greater use of free reading); (8) use of new technology and "systems," especially computerized instruction, which might provide improved methods, materials, and staff in one unit; (9) administrative changes, such as reduction of class size and changes in school size, and flexible programming of schedules through computers; (10) improved student incentives such as the use of money rewards for achievement, and improved participation, responsibility, and sense of meaning and power for students; and (11) increases in the numbers of students in school and the length of time spent there, especially in secondary and higher education.

EDUCATIONAL MILIEU. One likely possibility to be weighed is that schools may contribute less to the education of the young than nonschool factors, including voluntary reading, mass media, work, travel, voluntary group membership, military experience. Improved school achievement scores during this century may, indeed, be more a product of these factors than of the schools. So influential are the mass media in transmitting knowledge and values that Marshall McLuhan claims they are creating a social revolution as significant as was the printing press in the rise of Western man.[19] The new mass book market,

---

[19] Marshall McLuhan, *Understanding Media: The Extensions of Man* (New York: McGraw-Hill, 1964).

including about 400 million paperbacks sold annually, also contributes to learning. As for other formal sources, about ten million people take part in institutional adult education courses held by a variety of nonschool and school groups. It is estimated that more people are enrolled in courses in industry than in higher education. In the United States Armed Forces in 1955, some 6,000 courses from fifth grade thorugh the university were offered, and 122,600 earned eighth grade certificates in the Army. During the Second World War, a majority of some 300,000 illiterates were organized into special training units in the Army and brought up to fourth-grade literacy within 60 to 90 days. This improved educational milieu may make schools obsolete, or at least greatly change what they do. Both formal and informal education outside the schools may offer superior means of instruction than what can or will be offered in schools.

THE FAMILY. Roles of the family and school in educating and "socializing" the young and influencing and changing each other need further analysis. Increased intimacy between school and family is believed by some to be the primary means of improving student performance.

THE COMMUNITY. Some observers believe that the entire school community must be understood and its resources improved—including housing, recreation, and community organization—in order to affect student performance significantly.

SOCIETY. As previous chapters have indicated, the political and economics systems of a society, as well as their power structures, value systems, ideologies, and modes of stratification all greatly influence the schools and what happens to students in them.

INTERNATIONAL. The interaction of schools and student performance with international societies is virtually unexplored, but such interaction is very much in the future of American schools and society. Massive work-study programs of American students abroad (perhaps costing no more than is spent in schools here) may, for example, do more to promote desirable change in the educational and world communities than any other strategy of change.

ISOLATION VERSUS INTEGRATION. In the past the schools have been seriously isolated from family, community, American society, and international societies. Integrating school and life and bringing education into the social mainstream offers one important strategy of change.

Prospects

It is the promise of educational R&D that offers some hope of upgrading education. As we have seen, the past record is rather dismal. When the impact of research on the schools is calculated, the product may even be a negative one. The responsibility for this may be equally shared between scholars—who have given too much weight to the deficits of individuals and too little to the deficits of institutions and the social order—and schoolmen—who have often simply looked for scientific evidence to support their own views or deal with minor housekeeping issues.

Dan Dodson comments on the record of research:

> In the name of scientifically tested hypothesis clichés such as "low I.Q.," "low social class," "weak ego strength," "matriarchal domination," "cultural

118

deprivation," are propounded. The most current stereotype now being formed is about the dire necessity for these children to experience early preschool stimulation. The greatest task of the little man of our times will be to beat down the mythologies which the scholars have created about him. The educators have been seduced with the mystique of science. It should be remembered that the great documents by which we live are involved with the issues of their day, and had the ability to quicken the spirit and offer hope to the masses that there was a greater selfhood yet to be achieved.[20]

This has been the record of researchers who have been concerned with the child's psyche or management of traditional schools. The prospects for research concerned with changes in institutions, society and social policy seem more hopeful.

[20] Dan Dodson, *New Frontiers in Education* (New York: Greene & Stratton, 1966), pp. 300–302.

selected

references

Several dozen texts in the sociology of education exist. The reader is referred to books listed under the heading "educational sociology" in *Books in Print* for a list of all but the most dated volumes. The more recent and useful texts include: Jean D. Grambs, *Schools, Scholars, and Society* (Prentice-Hall, 1965); Robert Havighurst and Bernice Neugarten, *Society and Education* (Allyn & Bacon, 1962); Charles Page, *Sociology and Contemporary Education* (Random House, 1964); Harold Hodgkinson, *Education, Interaction, and Social Change* (Prentice-Hall, 1967); Wilbur Brookover and David Gottlieb, *A Sociology of Education* (American Book Co., 1964); Dorothy Westby-Gibson, *Social Foundations of Education* (Free Press, 1967); Ronald Corwin, *A Sociology of Education* (Appleton-Century-Crofts, 1965).

The works of James Bryant Conant are all significant because of their influence on educational policy. They have been concerned with problem solving and educational reform and all are brief and highly readable. Martin Mayer's *The Schools* (Harper, 1961) presents a comprehensive and critical survey of American education with considerable reference to schools abroad. Two volumes edited by Seymour Harris (McCutchen Press,

Berkeley, 1965) *Education and Public Policy* and *Challenge and Change in American Education* contain rich material on the economics of education.

The works of John Dewey are, of course, recommended as a background for many of the philosophic debates in American education. Paul Goodman's writings, including *Growing Up Absurd* (Random House, 1960), and Edgar Z. Friedenberg's writings, including *Coming of Age in America* (Random House, 1963), offer many provocative insights into the problems of growth and the schools. My own books, *Education and Income* (Viking, 1961) and *Spanish Harlem* (Harper & Row, 1965) deal with public policy issues, school stratification, and community as it affects schools.

Two major sources of detailed data about the nation's schools exist and are available to users for computer analysis. These are (1) data from *Project Talent* (Univ. of Pittsburgh), national follow-up study of twelfth graders; (2) the national survey of the nation's schools made by the U.S. Office of Education and summarized in *Equal Educational Opportunity*. Both the National Education Association and the U.S. Office of Education are major sources of information about public schools.

The publications of the American Educational Research Association (N.E.A.), including the *Encyclopedia of Educational Research*, report on research in education. *Sociology of Education* is the official education journal of the American Sociological Association. Comparative education material and the international studies that are reported are increasingly useful in studying the interaction of schools and society.

index